Prime Time

Prime Time

A GUIDE TO THE PLEASURES AND OPPORTUNITIES OF THE NEW MIDDLE AGE

Bernice Hunt and Morton Hunt

STEIN AND DAY/*Publishers*/New York

Names, locations, and certain unessential details
have been altered in the case histories to protect
the privacy of the individuals.

First published in 1975
Copyright © 1974 by Bernice Hunt and Morton Hunt
Library of Congress Catalog Card No. 74-79419
All rights reserved
Designed by Ed Kaplin
Printed in the United States of America
Stein and Day/*Publishers*/Scarborough House,
Briarcliff Manor, N.Y. 10510
ISBN 0-8128-1713-3

To our children, who,
though none of them believes it yet,
will one day be middle-aged—
and enjoy it.

ACKNOWLEDGMENTS

A number of organizations, and individuals associated with them, deserve our public thanks for assisting us in various ways in the gathering of information for this book. They include: the American Cancer Society; the Bureau of the Census of the U.S. Department of Commerce, and particularly Paul C. Glick and Arthur J.orton; the Bureau of Labor Statistics of the U.S. Department of Labor, and particularly Curtis L. Gilroy; the Employment Standards Administration of the U.S. Department of Labor; the Family Service Association of America; the Metropolitan Life Insurance Company; the National Institute of Mental Health of the U.S. Department of Health, Education, and Welfare; the Women's Bureau of the U.S. Department of Labor, and particularly Carmen R. Maymi. We also thank for their various suggestions and comments Professor Roger L. Gould of the University of California, Los Angeles; Dr. Daniel Krellenstein, research assistant professor of surgery at the Mount Sinai School of Medicine in New York; Dr. Leslie S. Libow of the Mount Sinai City Hospital Center in Elmhurst, New York; Professor Helena Z. Lopata, director of the Center for the Comparative Study of Social Roles of Loyola University of Chicago; and Dr. William H. Masters of the Reproductive Biology Research Foundation in St. Louis.

The table of marital coital frequencies in Chapter Four previously appeared in slightly different form in *Playboy* magazine, copyright © 1973 by *Playboy;* it previously appeared, in the same form as it does in this book, in *Sexual Behavior in the 1970s* (New York: Playboy Press, 1974), copyright © 1974 by Morton Hunt. The two tape-recorded interviews quoted in Chapter Four previously appeared, in part, in *Sexual Behavior in the 1970s,* and are here quoted in more complete form by permission of Playboy Press. Several other items from the survey reported in that same book, but previously unpublished, are used here by permission of the Playboy Foundation.

The *Journal of Gerontology* and Dr. Wayne Dennis have graciously permitted us to reprint, in adapted form, data which first appeared in the January 1966 issue, p. 106, in an article by Dr. Dennis.

The staff of the East Hampton Free Library has been both gracious and untiring in its efforts to borrow needed materials for us and to answer our innumerable queries.

Our largest debt is to those people we cannot thank by name—the many friends, acquaintances, and strangers who submitted to our inquiries and interviews, and who gave us so clear a picture of our subject.

Contents

Prime Time

1 *Middle Age Becomes Beautiful*

RECENT MEDICAL, PSYCHOLOGICAL,
AND SOCIAL DEVELOPMENTS THAT
HAVE CREATED THE NEW MIDDLE AGE

Quietly, unobtrusively, but unquestionably, middle age has been undergoing a revolution. During the past generation, for the first time in the modern era (and probably for the first time in human history), middle age has become, potentially, one of the best periods of life.

This is no rationalization, no wishful thinking such as has typified most previous advice and encouragement offered to those who are growing older. What follows is a factual report on the unprecedented changes that are currently altering the medical, psychological, and social aspects of middle age, and giving it a greater potential for pleasure, freedom, and self-fulfillment than any other period in the life cycle.

It would be absurd to pretend that the New Middle Age has all the advantages of youth; it does not. It does retain more of them today than it used to—but what is far more important, it now has a combination of advantages of its own that it never had before, and that no other time of life has. The facts we are about to present show that, in the modern context, middle age is or can be a wonderful, pleasurable, and wholly special time—the Prime Time of life. This book is addressed to all those who are anywhere from just under 40 to 65 and who have not yet become aware of the revolution that has been taking place in middle age, or who have not yet discovered how to make its victories their own.

The present chapter presents the highlights of our report; the subsequent chapters will go into more detail about each topic.

Not so many years ago, men and women approaching 40 felt that they were about to pass their prime; they were crossing the watershed of life beyond which all would be downhill.

Typically, the woman who had been a mother and homemaker up to that point was depressed by the prospect of her last child's imminent departure from home. She was soon to lose her leading role, and she had no substitute role or purpose in life ready at hand; she was about to become useless and therefore worthless. At the same time, she was worrying about the well-known ills of menopause awaiting her, and about her graying hair and thickening waistline. Middle age was hard upon her, and it stretched out ahead as a long winter of discontent, a time of ill health and waning self-respect, of aimlessness and boredom, to be gotten through by means of hobbies and bridge games, phone calls and redecorating, visits to doctors and department stores.

As much as anything else, the middle-aged woman worried about her relationship with her husband, who seemed to have little interest in anything but his work and regularly fell asleep in his chair after dinner, or who, perhaps, was away a great deal on business—a situation that tormented her with fears that he was involved with a younger woman (and, quite honestly, sex at home *had* been dull for a long time and was growing less and less frequent).

Her husband may indeed have had younger women on his mind (at the very least) because of late his wife had so often been gloomy and depressed, or irritable and demanding. Besides, he was troubled about the loss of his own youth, vigor, and attractiveness. His hair was getting a trifle gray or thin, he was having difficulty keeping his bit of a paunch from getting larger, and he was uncomfortably aware that he seemed to have far less interest in sex with his wife than he used to. He wondered whether his powers were waning—or whether, with another and younger woman (assuming one would find him acceptable), he would still be his old self.

All these concerns paralleled and intensified his other and perhaps deeper-rooted worries about growing middle-aged: although, unlike his wife, he did not face the imminent loss of his identity and major purpose in life, he saw himself as having reached the high point in his career because he had run out of time in which to achieve any greater success. He felt that he was all he would ever be, and that, indeed, he was about to start on a downward course; from now on, his life would be a long, inevitable descent toward the emptiness and idleness of retirement, old age, and death.

Such were the stereotypes of middle age only a generation or less ago. You may not have noticed, but people who fit these stereotypes are getting hard to find of late. The old *concept* of middle age is almost as prevalent as ever—but, oddly, people who embody the concept are not.

In this era of liberated womanhood, many women—perhaps most—look forward eagerly to the marvelous freedom of what used to be called, rather depressingly, "the empty nest." They have little reason to be depressed by it, and much reason to find it appealing. For one thing, more wives over 40 work now than ever before; with a new (or continuing) career and a new *raison d'être* to look forward to, the woman approaching middle age is largely relieved of the worries about her role that plagued her predecessor. She is freed of still other cares by recent medical developments which have robbed menopause of much of its physical menace. And having a better image of herself both as a person and as female, she is less apprehensive about her husband's interest in other women—and is herself more apt to remain sexually vital.

Similarly, far fewer men than formerly now see the beginning of middle age as the crest beyond which all roads lead downward. Recent studies by sociologists have shown that in their 40's, better-educated and occupationally higher-placed men are more optimistic and forward-looking about their careers and their personal lives than men with less education and lower occupational status. And since a constantly increasing proportion of our population has been going to college and either entering the professions or doing highly skilled kinds of work, an ever larger proportion of men has come to view mid-life as a time of continuing growth, achievement, and personal well-being. As for the waning of their sexual powers, most men are now aware, thanks to the many reports on recent sex-research findings in the mass media, that this problem is more apt to be in the head than in the gonads. But today, fewer middle-aged husbands have reason to be worried about the problem in the first place: a national survey published in 1974 reports that as part of our national sexual liberation from puritanical attitudes, contemporary middle-aged husbands and wives make love a great deal more often and with considerably more variety and freedom than did middle-aged husbands and wives only a generation ago, when Alfred Kinsey and his colleagues were making their historic survey of American sexual behavior.

Thus, middle age is psychologically a healthier period than it used to be. But it's also medically a healthier period. Thanks to recent research which has made us aware of the life-saving value of proper diet and adequate exercise, most middle-aged men and women are trimmer and more physically active than their predecessors. As one concrete result, the death rate from heart attack has begun to decline. The use of antibiotics and other major developments in medical care have greatly reduced the cumulative debilitating effects of infectious diseases, and public-school education in mouth care has produced a crop of middle-aged people who, unlike their parents, still have all or most of their own teeth. People in mid-life today are, by and large, physically still young, or at least youthful—and, more to the point, most of them *think* young or youthful. The good, gray, somber parents of our childhood—whose life expectancy was not much less than our own, but whose feelings about their own middle age were so negative, so defeatist—are all but gone.

Equally important are certain pervasive social developments that have profoundly altered the nature of middle age. People used to marry later and have larger families than they do now, and they were occupied by parental obligations well into mid-life; by the time their children had gone, there were few years left for the parents. But in the past several generations, the parental phase of life has been ending earlier and earlier—about half a dozen years earlier, by now. The typical middle-aged mother had her last child by the time she was 31, and the typical mother just coming up on middle age had hers by or before 30. Since most children, these days, live away from home by 18, most parents are only in their late 40's when the last child leaves home (fully half of them, in fact, are *younger* than that when this event takes place); they can therefore look forward to something like two and a half decades of married life as a childless couple. Clearly, most of these postparental couples like being a twosome, for they avoid having others live with them; it used to be common for middle-aged couples to house maiden sisters, bachelor brothers, widowed aunts or uncles, or their own aging parents, but today the practice is very rare.

And so in middle age, husband and wife are alone together once again—and many of them find this a renewing and wonderful situation. For one thing, in recent years, the classic feeling that sexual passion was improper or ridiculous in people beyond the child-bearing years has been quietly dying out along with many other sexual taboos. So after many years of marital sex flawed by fears that the children might barge into the bedroom unexpectedly or were listening on the other side of a partition wall, the middle-aged couple is apt to find their new privacy heady and liberating. Many of them rediscover sexual pleasure and behave with greater freedom, spontaneity, and exuberance than they have in twenty years. Some even find their sex lives more exciting and satisfying than they were before they had children.

The absence of children and others in the home also makes for renewed and deepened intimacy of other kinds. This is a time of life when many husbands and wives rediscover what it is like to talk to each other and to share every thought and feeling. This is a time when they can dare to voice their private dreams—and are more nearly free than ever to try to make them come true. This is a time when they are far better able than they were during active parenthood to break through the cultural prohibitions against pleasure-seeking; a time when, together, they can travel, meet and make new friends, learn new skills, pursue ambitions, fulfill long-held aspirations—all with more freedom, time, and money than they have ever had before.

Freedom, yes—but do middle-aged couples really have more money than ever? Indeed they do: the survey data show that their income is at a peak and their expenses are sharply down. As compared with the earlier years of adulthood, mid-life is a period of relative affluence, even under the present conditions of inflation and economic slowdown. Moreover, the dramatic growth of federal and private retirement programs, and of other forms of financial security in old age, has liberated the middle-aged from their former obsession with scrimping and saving for the future.

Do people in mid-life really have noticeably more time? Absolutely; they have more time than ever—enough to start and complete much that they have long dreamed of, and much that they have never dared to dream of. For raising a family, establishing a career, and amassing material possessions require an enormous amount of each day's time—time which now, in middle age, can be reallocated and used to add to the store of one's self. For the first time since their own childhood, parents can be largely inner-directed, employing their newly released time and energy to develop the ego-pleasing and ego-satisfying facets of their own personalities and helping their mates to do the same.

Beyond each individual's particular ambitions and special pleasures, middle age, by its very nature, makes available a variety of ego gratifications—if one is able to welcome and make the most of the new roles mid-life brings with it. For middle age is a time of *maturity*—a state that is not opposed to continuing youthfulness, but that offers a wealth of satisfactions which are simply not available to the young. It is deeply gratifying to see oneself (and to know that others do, too) as wise, self-assured, dignified, and understanding. And best of all, comfortable in all kinds of situations, for there are few situations the middle-aged person has never encountered before.

To function in the role of mature human being with belief and inner conviction, we need to reexamine ourselves and to replace those ideas, aims, and behavior patterns that are not presently appropriate to our time of life or to the person we have become; that may mean discarding many old habits, tastes, beliefs, even friendships that no longer fit us—a difficult and possibly painful process. But having done it, and having made new selections that do fit, we will find the new self—the mature self—satisfying, and its time of life a truly Prime Time.

A first step in realizing the potentialities of middle age is to dispose of certain long-established misconceptions which are still widely held even though they do not stand up under scientific scrutiny, or which may once have been true but no longer are so under contemporary conditions.

Perhaps the most important misconception is the idea that arrival at middle age is a crisis. There may be—and should be—a distinct experience of *transition* in becoming middle-aged, but not every transition is a crisis. Indeed, some recent studies indicate that today, for most people, the stresses associated with reaching middle age are not critical, and that the transitions to certain other stages of life are commonly just as stressful, if not more so. Innumerable people have found it more difficult to become 14 than 40.

It is certainly true that for some, the transition to middle age is painful, frightening, and even destructive; these are the people who are unprepared to assume their new roles, people whose very identity and value depend on youthful beauty or athletic ability, people who still believe all the old depressing traditions about middle age. But it is their own value systems, and not the actual conditions of middle age, that are responsible for their experiencing this juncture as a crisis.

Other misconceptions center around the several myths that hold middle age to be a time of waning mental and sexual powers and of failing emotional and mental health. The evidence to be reviewed in subsequent chapters of this book shows the truth to be otherwise. There is no overall loss of learning ability and no decline in intelligence during middle age. Sexually, time brings some physiological changes, but these can be easily compensated for by proper knowledge of technique and by proper medication; there need be no lessening of sexual satisfaction in middle age, nor an ending of sexual activity for either sex before the late 70's or even the 80's. Physical health in mid-life is generally adequate to good, and most physical capacities diminish little before the late 60's. As for mental health, while there is a steady increase in the incidence of psychosis, this affects only a very tiny percentage even of those who are in their mid-60's; what is still more reassuring is that neuroses, which are far more common, do not become more prevalent during middle age.

If all this is so, why aren't the middle-aged happy? Most of them *are;* it's only the tradition that says they're not. Surveys made a generation or more ago found that most people rated their earlier years as having been the happiest or most satisfying, but more recently other surveys have shown a change: substantial proportions—and in some surveys, majorities—of older people rate the middle years as having been the best part of their lives. But while they have said so privately to sociologists, they apparently have not said it publicly to the world around them. Their silence, we think, is due to the dampening effect of tradition, which has viewed youth as the time of greatest happiness, and has regarded it as foolish, undignified, and unsuitable for the middle-aged person to behave as if he were, or to claim to be, intensely happy.

The negative view of middle age and the even more negative one of old age is a part of our own cultural heritage, but not that of all peoples. Age has long been honored and revered throughout the Orient, and in traditional China the retired older person was thought to have arrived at the richest and most enjoyable part of life. In cultures such as the Balinese and Hindu, where it is believed that one goes on after death through an intervening period and then to a reincarnation, advancing age is seen not as a deterioration and ending but as progress toward a worthy goal and as an important stage of a continuing process.

In primitive societies, too, there is little or none of the obsessive concern with one's chronological age that is so common in Western civilization. In these simpler and more stable societies older people have been treasured for the many special roles they take—those of baby-sitters and surrogate parents, storytellers, preservers of oral tradition and custom, performers of rituals and magic, teachers of valuable knowledge, and, above all, makers of important decisions. In such a setting, people have no reason to dread birthdays; they know that they will continue to occupy important, honored, and powerful places in society until they are well into senescence.

In Western civilization, however, the tradition has been quite different. From the time of Alexander the Great on, poets have worshiped youth, mourned its passing, and vilified the coming of age; only an occasional elderly philosopher has sought to argue the case for the rewards of growing old. In compilations such as Stevenson's *Quotations* there are numerous celebrations of youth and condemnations of age but almost nothing to the contrary. Most curious of all is the fact that in over two thousand years very few people have ever written about middle age by way of either praise or condemnation, for in our culture it has not been seen as a separate and special time of life. There was only youth and, when that was gone, old age. One quotation—a good one, attributed to Shakespeare—will serve to exemplify the tradition:

> Crabbed age and youth cannot live together;
> Youth is full of pleasance, age is full of care;
> Youth like summer morn, age like winter weather;
> Youth like summer brave, age like winter bare.
> Youth is full of sport, age's breath is short;
>   Youth is nimble, age is lame;
> Youth is hot and bold, age is weak and cold;
>   Youth is wild, and age is tame.
> Age, I do abhor thee; youth, I do adore thee . . .
>   —*The Passionate Pilgrim*

And when on rare occasions someone did take notice of middle age, it was to see it only as a brief and meaningless time of transition from youth to age. This, at least, was Byron's opinion of it:

> Of all the barbarous middle ages, that
>   Which is most barbarous is the middle age
> Of man; it is—I really scarce know what;
>   But when we hover between fool and sage.
>   —*Don Juan,* xii, 1

This tradition has had particular force in the United States. Ours has been a youth-oriented culture since its beginnings, and for good reason. In the early years of our nation's existence, it was a place where only the young could survive, let alone thrive. In 1776, when the Declaration of Independence was written, half the people in the nation were under 16, and three quarters under 25. It took muscle and stamina to clear the forests, to wring a living from the untamed earth, to survive harsh winters in primitive conditions, to deal with hostile Indians. With some notable exceptions—Ben

Franklin, of course, comes to mind—most of the makers and shapers of the new society were relatively young or, at most, in their early middle age.

Such was the tradition of our early years. Later, with the westward expansion, it was reinforced; still later, with the burgeoning of technology, the tradition was strengthened yet again, for only the young, and particularly those fresh from college or technical training, could understand and deal with the new machinery, tools, and procedures that were transforming American life. And by that time, a large part of the population consisted of immigrants who were, at best, imperfectly "Americanized," and who clung to their old ways and ideas; their children, the young second-generation Americans, were at once their hope, their teachers, and their leaders.

Things are different now. We are no longer instantly old, or dead, the moment we pass beyond youth. Not only is our life expectancy far greater than that of Americans of a century ago, but for reasons we offered earlier, the middle-aged of today are not as old, physically or psychologically, as were the middle-aged of only a generation ago. And while society is changing as rapidly as ever, the adults who are now entering, or are in the midst of middle age, are a generation who were more highly trained by their society and its educational system—and, above all, trained to be flexible and adaptable. We have known and lived with the unpredictable future all along: change has been the most stable feature of our lives.

The worst thing about contemporary middle age is that it ends not with a bang but a whimper. It leads to old age, and not even those who make the most of middle age look forward to being aged, for old age does finally bring enfeeblement, degenerative disorders, the death of people we love, the imminence of our own death. Still, most of us have absorbed some of the attitudes implicit in the pervasive modern philosophy of ecology, in which all of these changes are seen as natural and normal, as part of life, and not as failure or tragedy. But even without consciously adopting such attitudes, we will meet and experience old age calmly and without regret if we have made our youth and especially our middle age rich and fulfilling, for then we will not feel that death is cheating us of what we should have had and never did. The philosopher-psychoanalyst Erik Erikson says that for the person who has experienced real "generativity"—who has been the originator of others, or the generator of products and ideas—old age is a time of "ego integrity" rather than despair: a time when, fulfilled, one attains "the gift of responsible renunciation" and "a detached concern with life itself, in the face of death itself." This special satisfaction, in the eighth and final stage of life (in Erikson's view), is dependent upon the richness and fullness with which the preceding stages—especially the seventh, or next-to-last, stage—have been lived.

In other words, those who live life fully and creatively in middle age will arrive at old age without feeling short-changed and without despair or anger, but with a sense of completion, fitness, and fullness. The richer, more expansive, and more creative one's middle age, the more acceptable and tranquil will be the end of one's life.

And now, we, the authors of this book, would like to tell you a little about why we wanted to write it, and about ourselves. To some extent, these two things are one and the same.

We are both in our mid-50's, and our respective children are grown and on their own. That's typical for our age bracket, but in some ways we are not exactly the typical middle-aged couple. We met the summer we were 17, knew each other very briefly before going off to college, and did not meet again until we were in our mid-40's; then we became close friends and frequently saw each other socially, together with our spouses. But after some years, Bernice was widowed and Morton was divorced, both within a half year. Until then, it had never crossed our minds that we might be anything other than dear friends—and then one day it *did* cross our minds. We were married shortly thereafter.

While our marriage has not been a lengthy one to date, it has been rich in experience, both in itself and in the dowry of previous experiences each of us has brought to the partnership. We came to each other directly from terribly traumatic events, and could easily have fallen into a thoroughly neurotic relationship, but that isn't what happened. For through patience, understanding, and the sharing of every thought and emotion, and with the insights each of us had earlier gained from psychoanalysis, we have been able to build a relationship as intimate, complete, and satisfying as any we could ever have hoped for. We quarrel from time to time, we weep occasionally, but we laugh a good deal, are glad to start and to end each day together, enjoy and share a wide variety of interests and activities, and love each other very much. But we do not "live in each other's pockets"; each of us has his or her own work, activities, and individual identity, each of us respects the other's need for privacy, each of us has absolute trust in the other and feels no need to place artificial limits on the other's freedom in order to feel secure.

We can each say, with absolute honesty, that this is the happiest time of our lives—but we can't personally take all the credit. Largely responsible are the special characteristics of the time in which we live that give middle age such unprecedented potential. What has been possible for us would not have been so at some earlier time—but what is so for us today is in large part possible for everyone.

We wanted to tell you this much about ourselves because even though our history as a couple is hardly typical, the sum of our experiences is: accordingly, our encounter with middle age, our solutions to its problems, and our enjoyment of its manifold possibilities can be matched by nearly any couple with the same information and preparedness. We do not consider ourselves gurus, but we feel confident that most people, without trying to do the very same things we do, but thinking along the same general pathways and modifying their behavior to fit their own special needs, can make middle age their Prime Time.

2 Health, Money, Love— and Time to Enjoy Them

SOME OF THE ASSETS THAT ACCRUE IN MIDDLE AGE

The Spanish toast that serves as the title of this chapter is an ideal summary of what middle age can offer—especially, and perhaps surprisingly, the last of the good wishes—time to enjoy the first three. In this chapter, we won't have much to say about love (although we'll have a lot to say about it later on), but we do want to talk about health and money, and most of all about time; it is of the utmost importance to recognize that mid-life, now, offers far more time to enjoy things, both in terms of years ahead and in terms of the available hours in each day, than it offered only a generation ago.

Let's start with the years that lie ahead of us. Today, the white American male at age 40 has, on the average, a life expectancy of another 32 years and the white female at age 40 has an average life expectancy of another 38 years. (Nonwhite males and females have, respectively, 4 and 4½ fewer years.) The big leap in life expectancy came before the turn of the century, but even in the past three decades it has kept increasing: the figures above represent a two-year increase for men, and a four-and-a-half-year increase for women, just since 1940, and increases of nearly twice that much since 1900. And as you get further into middle age, time keeps stretching out ahead of you: the closer you get to the average age of death, the better your chances of beating the average. In simple numbers, it looks like this:

AVERAGE EXPECTATION OF LIFE IN YEARS *

	White Males	*Total Life Expectancy*	*White Females*	*Total Life Expectancy*
At age 40	32 more	72	38 more	78
At age 50	23 more	73	29 more	79
At age 65	13 more	78	17 more	82

So a man of 40 can expect to reach 72, and a woman of 40 can expect to reach 78—and a man of 65 can look forward not to just another 7 years but another 13, while a woman of 65 can look forward not to 13 more years but to 17 more.

Thus, as you enter middle age you have many years ahead of you—nearly half of your life, *and well over half of your adult life.* Middle age isn't the leftover tag end of life; it's a very major part of it. It would be too bad if, not realizing this, you didn't do your best to enjoy it.

An examination of the difference in the average life expectancies of men and women does, however, bring up one painful matter—the threat of widowhood in middle age. All of us have known a few widowers and many widows who are in their middle years; we may think of middle age as involving the constant risk of widowhood and its loneliness and other miseries. There is no point in pretending this is without reality—but it was more true in the past than the present. When we look at the actual figures, it turns out that today, the chance that a married couple will live, intact, through middle age is several times as great as the chance that one or the other will die before 65. For instance, for every man in the 55-to-64 age bracket who is a widower, 25 others are married; and for every woman in the 55-to-64 age bracket who is a widow, more than three are married. Hence, while we will have many things to

* Adapted from *Statistical Abstract of the United States, 1973,* Table 795, rounded off to the nearest decimal place.

say which apply to the single, the divorced, and the widowed, the main focus of this book will be on middle-aged couples, for middle age is, above all, a period when people live in couples.

So there's a lot of time left. But, you might ask, will you be healthy enough to enjoy living those many years? One of the things that make many people fear middle age is the belief that it is a period when one will inevitably be plagued by chronic diseases and conditions. How many times have you said, as you came down from a ladder, "I must be getting old—I can feel my knees creak." Or, "It won't be long before I need a Seeing-Eye Dog—I can't even look up a number in the telephone directory without my glasses." Or, "I can't seem to handle rich food (or whiskey, or late parties, or three flights of stairs) the way I used to." It's a natural step from these observations to the dire conclusion that in middle age the mortal flesh becomes heir to innumerable degenerative processes and chronic ailments such as asthma, bronchitis, diabetes, nervous and mental disorders, malfunctions or diseases of the circulatory, respiratory, digestive, and genitourinary systems, arthritis and rheumatism, and impairments of sight and hearing.

Well, don't leap to any such conclusion. Your knees probably do creak once in a while; most middle-aged people need glasses to read fine print; and most of us past 40 do have to take it somewhat easier with rich foods, alcohol, late hours, stairways, and the like. But that doesn't mean that your life is about to be spoiled by a series of disabling ailments. It is true that some of the chronic conditions listed above are more common in middle age than in the earlier years—but not so much more so, as most people suppose. It may surprise you to know that, according to figures published by the Metropolitan Life Insurance Company, two fifths of all people between the ages of 15 and 44 already have one or more of these chronic conditions, and that between the ages of 45 and 64 the figure reaches only three fifths; while that is a sizable increase, it is hardly a grave or depressing one.

There is, to be sure, a particularly sharp increase in the circulatory and respiratory diseases, arthritis, and rheumatism, and the beginning of a steady climb in the incidence of cancer, but each of these ailments still affects only small minorities of the middle-aged;

it is only beyond the mid-60's that the rates begin to soar. Incidentally, some of the other chronic diseases—notably asthma, chronic bronchitis, and peptic ulcer—level off (or even decline) in incidence during middle age. So does the loss of visual accommodation (near vision), which begins to level off at about age 55 and does not decline further after 60.

In any case, of those persons in the 45-to-64 group who do have chronic conditions, Metropolitan Life found that only one man in seven and one woman in eight are limited in the performance of their major activities, whether these consist of working at a job, keeping house, attending school, or whatever. Most important of all, chronic conditions render fewer than 3 per cent of all men and women in that age group wholly incapable of carrying out their major activities.

So we see that most persons entering middle age have plenty of time ahead—good time, time without disabling illness. Let's turn now to the other aspect of time—the number of hours per day in which one is free to follow the heart's desire. Middle age brings an immense liberation of this kind of time, too, for both men and women.

Turn back the clock for a moment to try to recall what happened to the hours of your day when you became a parent. According to various studies, the presence of children adds about forty-five hours of work per week of child care and extra housework (most of which has always fallen upon the mother), and this added work load remains much the same until the youngest child is well into the teens. The change in daily routine when the children finally move away and the regaining of freedom to use the day's waking hours for oneself again are so obvious that they require no proof. Yet because it happens gradually, we forget; let's look back for a moment, so that we can appreciate how different life is now:

Bernice comments

The average day began with the breakfast rush, the packing of three school lunches, trying to find a lost shoe, and getting everybody out in time to meet the school bus. A *worse* than average day began when a frantic search for last night's homework turned up the dog-chewed remains under the sofa; by the time the tears were dried and a note written to the teacher, the bus had come and gone with only two aboard, so Mother was dashing off to drive the other one to school—if it happened to be a day when the car would start.

On good days, between doing laundry, straightening up the house, marketing, and cooking, there were at most a couple of hours set aside for myself, when I could write—and then, before I knew it, it was three o'clock and I was off on the full round of the suburban mother's taxi service: dentist, Scouts, ballet lesson, play rehearsal—then back to pick them all up again, the logistics requiring the skills of a four-star general.

Saturdays from 9 A.M. to 1 P.M. were spent at the Manhattan School of Music (with forty minutes of driving each way) to wait through one piano lesson, one violin lesson, one flute lesson, and everybody's theory class and Music Hour.

Aside from all this, and going as class mother on trips, baking for bazaars, handling the usual meals, hassles, homework problems, illnesses, birthday parties, and the hundreds of other odds and ends, my time was all my own.

Don't get me wrong. It was a happy time, a wonderful time, and one I wouldn't have missed for anything in the world. It even paid off because those three children grew up to be three remarkably nice people. It was all fine while I did it; I knew that my time belonged to my family then because that was the way I had planned it, and wanted it, and the way it had to be. But when it was over, it was fantastic to have all those hours belong to me again.

Time is in short supply for fathers, too. No one, as far as we know, has studied the average weekly work load that children impose on fathers, and it is difficult to make a meaningful estimate because the variations within families are enormous. But even a relatively preoccupied or minimal Dad helps, to some extent or other, with the extra housework required by the presence of children—more in these egalitarian days than ever—and, presumably, nearly every father puts in some amount of time directly with his children, reading bedtime stories to the preschooler and helping the school kids with homework; taking the children to ball games, the circus, the movies, concerts, the beach, picnics; playing ball with them, helping them make things, teaching them to ride a two-wheeler. Beyond all that, there are the many dull hours spent at PTA meetings, Scout meetings, open house at the school, the senior play, and—well, you name it. You've been there.

Yet that is the least of it. The father's main time-consumer is the career push, the need to "make it," the drive to work longer, or harder, or to moonlight, in order to be able to afford the bigger house, set aside money for college, pay for all those shoes, shirts, jeans, athletic jackets, music lessons, visits to the orthodontist, summers at camp. We recall one friend who said with mixed wonder and regret when he was in his mid-30's, "I don't understand it—just a few years ago I was a carefree, happy young guy, and now I have this whole establishment depending on me. I'm completely boxed in—and I don't even know how it all happened."

But once the children have grown up and left home, the man can finally ease off, stop being primarily a source of supply, pay some attention to his own desires, spend more time with his wife, and rediscover—or discover for the first time—the delights of two-some selfishness.

Our friend Alex R., who has his own public relations office, used to arrive there well before 9 A.M. every day—ahead of his employees—and rarely left before 7 P.M. Dinners with out-of-town clients and evening conferences frequently kept him tied up until late; many a night by the time he got home Sue, his wife, weary from her own heavy workday as mother and homemaker, had gone to bed and was asleep. It was a rat race, and Alex didn't like it much—but he couldn't afford to lose an account or miss the chance to snag a new one, because every time he added up the family's expenses for the year they were more than last year's, and always beyond his estimate. When Alex was in a good mood, he often said that he felt like Alice in Wonderland, who had to run at top speed in order to stay in the same place; when he was in a bad mood, he didn't say anything.

In the last few years, though, things have changed. Both of their children have completed college and are now supporting themselves; Alex and Sue have sold the big house and replaced it by a four-room apartment and a cottage in the country; and Alex himself, for the first time in many years, has stopped worrying about money. His present list of clients provides him with a comfortable enough income for two people, and he doesn't solicit new accounts unless an old client leaves him. He now limits restaurant conferences to lunchtime, gets home before six every evening, and leaves the office early Friday afternoon in order to pick up Sue and beat the traffic out to the country. When Alex and Sue have friends to dinner at the cottage on Sunday night, or go to a party, they spend the night in the country and get back to the city around 11 A.M. on Monday; Alex's secretary copes until he gets there. Alex laughs more than he has for a long time; he's relaxed and yet excited about the things he's doing now—gardening, horseback riding, carpentry, traveling; and he's even talking about going back to complete the Ph.D. he abandoned many years ago.

Like Alex R., many men readjust their work drive in middle age, when the pressures on them diminish. But this does not mean that they jeopardize their jobs or even that they earn less—unless they deliberately plan to, as Alex did. In *Aging and Society*, a massive 1972 survey of recent research on every aspect of aging, sociologist Matilda White Riley and two associates cited one study which showed that job stability is particularly high in middle age: workers between the ages of 45 and 64 are less likely than younger persons either to lose their jobs or to leave them. As for income, the data are equally reassuring: whereas studies made at a Midwestern university a generation ago showed that the average American male's income peaked at 55 to 56 and then leveled off or declined, more recent data included in Dr. Riley's compendium show that income now tends to keep increasing right up to retirement.

To be sure, the inflation and the recession that are afflicting the American economy as we write these words have affected the middle-aged along with everyone else. But even in these difficult times, middle age is still—when compared with the preceding phase of life—a period when income is up, expenses sharply down, and prospects generally favorable.

The financial situation of the middle-aged is further strengthened by the fact that a large number of middle-aged wives—more than four out of every ten—are employed. This is part of the overall change in women's roles and outlook associated with women's liberation: twice as many married women work today as did in the late 1940's (42 per cent as compared with 20 per cent). It is still true—though not as true as formerly—that many married women stop working when the first child arrives, but as soon as the youngest child is even partially independent, these women begin to reenter the labor force. The latest figures from the Women's Bureau of the Department of Labor tell the story. Considering only married women who are living with their husbands (that is, omitting the separated, divorced, and widowed), 71 per cent of those who are under 25 years old and childless work, and if they remain childless, this figure increases, then drops slowly to 54 per cent by age 54. But most women do have children by their mid-20's—and from 71 per cent who work, the figure drops to 30 per cent for women of 25 to 34 with small children. Then, as the women and their children grow older, the women go back to work: between 35 and 44, even if they have children under 18, 46 per cent work, and from 45 to 54, if they have no children left under the age of 18, the figure rises to 54 per cent. Putting all this together, we get a life-cycle curve that looks like this:

PERCENTAGES OF MARRIED WOMEN WHO WORK *

Age and Motherhood Status	16–24 and Childless	25–44 and Children under 6	35–44 and Children under 18	45–54 and No Children under 18

Per cent

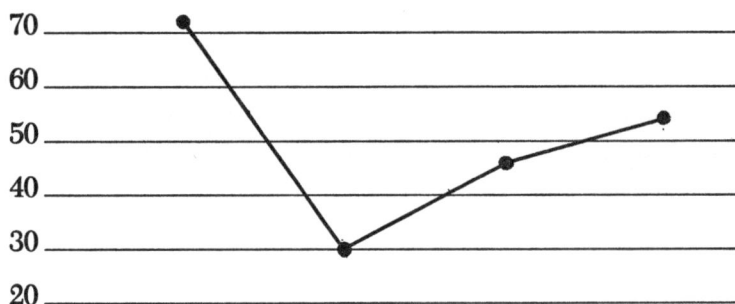

* Source: Women's Bureau, U.S. Department of Labor, 1972 data. In using figures from four different categories, we have tried to approximate the most typical pattern for present-day American women.

The return to work in middle age has much value for the married woman; it not only makes middle age a time of unprecedented financial comfort but through new responsibility and new income gives the woman a sense of added worth and importance. In addition, a job is a source of contact with new people and new stimuli, and provides the woman with a multifaceted new start in life. All this is well known and generally acknowledged; the chief difficulty today is not the woman's own reluctance to return to work, as was formerly the case, but that of employers to hire her.

The woman who worked all along, of course, has no problem, and the one who took off only a few years from a successful career should have relatively little trouble finding a job. But the woman who tries to return to work after twenty years of homemaking, or who in middle age seeks paid employment for the first time, may find it difficult to know where to look, and discouraging to learn that she seems to have no marketable talents. For these women, career counseling may provide good answers.

Career-counseling services come in many sizes and shapes, and it's up to you, if you need such help, to proceed cautiously in making a selection. Some are commercial, strictly-for-profit agencies; you'll find them listed in the classified phone book under such headings as "Career Guidance" and "Vocational Guidance." Some of these are excellent, some are merely in the business of selling expensive tests, workshops, and appraisals which have little real value. If anyone you know personally has had experience with these agencies, you may be able to get some information on which ones are worthwhile and which are not; you can also get some idea yourself by having a consultation session with the program director, reading the brochures, and checking on the credentials of the staff through professional directories in your local library.

Better yet, contact the nearest college or university and ask whether it has a vocational-guidance service; many do, and they can be trusted to do a good, nonprofit-oriented job. Even if it has no such career service, the psychology or social work department may be able to steer you in the right direction. So may your local women's organizations, or even your state employment agency.

The personnel in vocational-guidance services try to appraise the basic skills, the interests, and the life experiences of the client; this assessment—which some women can actually perform for themselves—turns up all sorts of marketable assets, particularly in the present climate of women's liberation when so many opportunities that would have been out of the question a while back are now opening up to women. Two quick examples of putting amateur experience to professional use:

Linda T., an acquaintance of ours, hadn't worked since her first child was born, but over the years she had become the neighborhood wonder with plants, both indoor and outdoor, and had made a hobby of reading up on horticultural science. She had never thought of that as a marketable asset, but as soon as it was suggested to her by a career counselor, she began to make the rounds of local nurseries. Rather soon, to her surprise and delight, she got a job in one of them and proved to be a valuable aid to the owners, since she was able to answer all of the common questions the customers asked and to make highly informed recommendations of specific plants or procedures suited to the customers' particular needs.

Margaret O., a longtime suburban housewife, ruefully told a counselor that she had become a mother immediately after completing her college education and had never worked; frankly, she said, she didn't believe she could do anything that anybody would be willing to pay for. But with a little probing, the counselor discovered that for the past several years Margaret had been raising funds for the local free library and had, in fact, gotten last year's annual contributions up to nearly $10,000—the largest sum in the library's history. The counselor suggested that she had the makings of a career in professional fund-raising for charity organizations, a job category Margaret had never even heard of before. After some searching, she became assistant to the fund-raiser for a large voluntary hospital in the city; now, after several years, she is highly experienced and expects to move into the senior job next year, when her boss retires.

All in all, with the continuing increase in the husband's income, the wife's return to work, and the end of the major financial burdens of parenthood, middle age is a time of relative affluence for most people. It is a matter of record that the middle-aged have fewer debts and more money in savings accounts than people in any other age bracket. Persons between 45 and 64 make up 30 per cent of the adult population but more than 40 per cent of the nation's stockholders, and the average age of persons with incomes of $15,000 and over is 51.

Thus, middle age today is a phase of the life cycle when health is good, or at least adequate, when there is more money than ever before, and when there is more time to enjoy one's self than there has been in many years. And middle-aged people *do* enjoy themselves—and each other. A survey by sociologist Leland J. Axelson of nearly five hundred postparental fathers and mothers found that people tended to rate their postparental lives as better in each of four major areas of inquiry than they had been when they still had at least one child in high school. Omitting those who saw no change, Axelson reported that men, by a margin of 5 to 1, and women by a margin of 10 to 1, said that financial worries had decreased rather than increased during the postparental period. By similarly impressive majorities, men and women reported increased activities with the spouse, and more satisfaction with marital adjustment. Even their daily work more often increased in interest than declined.

It is no accident that the largest margin of improvement in this survey dealt with the decrease of financial worries. Those of us who are middle-aged now can count ourselves fortunate that we have come to this part of life at this time in history, when, for many reasons, mid-life is so much freer of financial insecurity than it used to be. Most of us, especially those who were "Depression children," can recall how our parents—our fathers in particular—were eternally burdened with money worries, partly because of the problem of supporting us, far into their middle years, but also because of the uncertainty of their own futures. They talked all the time about saving for a "rainy day"—which, in part, meant illness or even harder times, but which, in larger part, was their euphemism for old age. And because they worried, they worked on Saturdays if they could, or at night, and put in as many as sixty hours a week so as to lay aside some security for that ever-imminent, ever-frightening future.

Morton comments

My father's occupation was somewhat special: he was an undertaker, which always seemed terribly funny to my friends and made our lives rather different from everybody else's. But in most ways, my father and my mother had the same problems and the same worries as most other middle-class parents of that time. Like many of their friends, they had started to have children later than most people do today, and then had run head on into the crisis of the Depression; and so they were still struggling every day when they were in their 40's and 50's with old, piled-up business debts and long-standing loans, with a house badly in need of plumbing repairs and repainting, with a hundred kinds of household and family expenses, each one of which seemed to be the straw that might break the camel's back.

My father hardly ever had time to enjoy himself all through his 40's and 50's; he was too busy trying to make ends meet. Many a night he was out attending boring business and club meetings in the hope of making good contacts. Once a week at most, he and my mother might play bridge with friends, and in the summer he would get to the beach with us a few times for an hour or two. Night after night he sat up in bed reading until 2 or 3 A.M., fearful of turning out the light because that was when the specter of business collapse and bankruptcy haunted him and his mind seethed with fears and worries. I don't remember seeing him smile or hearing him laugh much throughout my childhood.

When my sister and I had finally grown up and gone off on our own (and when, coincidentally, business conditions had improved greatly), my father and my mother at last had money enough to enjoy themselves. But it was too late: she was 59 and dying of cancer, and he was 68 and there was no time left. Yet he was lucky, after all: a year after my mother died, he married a wonderful, exuberant, loving woman, and had nearly five splendid years, with enough money for the two of them to do things he had always dreamed of. They crisscrossed the country, went to the theater and to concerts, played golf, saw a lot of their friends, fixed up a new apartment. But then time ran out; at 75, my father died. He had had five very good years, and that's better than none—but most of *my* friends were under 50 when they began to have the postparental advantages and had twenty or thirty years of the good life to look forward to. For them, and the two of us, middle age bears no resemblance to that of our parents; it has become, truly, the Prime Time of our lives.

We do, to be sure, live in better times than the 1930's and we do finish with parenthood earlier. But one of the most important factors in relieving today's middle-aged people of financial pressure and making their lives more enjoyable is something else altogether —namely, the large-scale social shift of responsibility for financial security in age or illness: instead of each person's bearing that burden by himself, it has been transferred to and spread out among government agencies, industry, unions, and insurance companies.

Social Security was born in 1935; it made a modest beginning, but in the four decades that have passed since then, it has expanded until it covers nearly all retired workers, severely disabled people, and wives, widows, and children of retired, disabled, or deceased workers. Benefits are also available for dependent husbands and widowers, surviving dependent parents, and surviving divorced wives and widows. One in eight Americans receives a monthly Social Security check, and the size of the payments has increased steadily over the years. In addition, a recent change in the law has made Social Security payments inflation-proof so that they will not shrink in buying power if prices continue to rise.

During recent decades, many other developments similarly designed to transfer responsibility from the individual to social institutions have gone still further to lessen the concern of the middle-aged that they might be impoverished later. Group pension and retirement plans of various sorts have burgeoned until most employed people are covered by employer-provided or cooperative retirement plans. Individual retirement plans and postponed-tax (Keogh Plan) funds are available to self-employed workers. Insurance companies, responding to the national mood, have offered a wealth of new forms of protection against the hazards of age—most notably, insurance against hospital and medical bills, and the loss of income during illness. The federal government further protects us against the high medical costs of age through the Medicare program of the Social Security Administration, which provides hospital insurance for almost everyone over 65, and, for those who choose to pay a small premium, insurance against doctors' bills as well. For those who are in genuine financial distress, moreover, the Medicaid program—funded jointly by the federal Department of Health, Education, and Welfare and the various states, and operated by state health or welfare agencies—pays in-hospital and outpatient bills, doctors' bills, the cost of nursing care, and so on. (These various private and public health insurance programs seem very likely to be supplemented or superseded in the next couple of years by some form of national health insurance.)

While it is true that the payments from these several sources will not provide us with a sumptuous life-style in our late years, it is also true that they are sufficient to have wrought a revolution in our outlook on earning and spending in middle age: most of us no longer worry about someday being unable to pay our bills, becoming charity cases on public welfare or in our children's homes, or being unable to afford visits to the doctor or costly operations. The kind of security we have today would have made a vast difference in the way our parents lived their middle age.

In contrast to the people of the preceding generation, we can afford to luxuriate in middle age; freed from their chronic anxiety and insecurity, we can indulge ourselves in sports, socializing, travel, study, political involvement, and a host of other activities that we have been meaning to, or wanting to, find time for. And as we shift the emphasis from work and parental duty toward more avocational and recreational activities we are not engaging in thoughtless self-indulgence; the shift is a valuable adaptation to our changed present and a priceless preparation for our future. For it is a demonstrated fact that men and women who make such a transition early in middle age are the ones who, many years later, are the most generally successful in their retirement years. Those, on the other hand, who remain nose-to-grindstone until they are 65 are likely to become depressed, withdrawn, crotchety, ailing, and disoriented when they abruptly cease to be the storekeeper, designer, supervisor, forewoman, sales manager, private secretary, or judge, and have nothing to do, nothing to *be*. Rehearsal for retirement should begin in middle age. But the rehearsal isn't solely a matter of learning how to play, for of itself play isn't good enough. This may seem an odd statement when nearly every magazine and newspaper we pick up offers glowing advertisements for retirement paradises where the sun always shines, the grounds are kept immaculate by employees, and one need do nothing but fish, swim, play shuffleboard, and loaf. All of which is held up to view as a kind of return to Eden, an ideal way of life, which indeed it may sometimes seem to those who are hard at work and longing for a vacation; the truth, though, is that man (or woman) cannot live by play alone. Full-time play is satisfying only for small children, for it is a major part of their primary business, learning; as one of our own children said at age four, "Playing is my work." But full-time play cannot provide sufficient psychic reward, self-esteem, or a sense of the importance of one's activities to adults who have long been engaged in socially valuable and necessary functions.

In middle age—and all the more later on, after retirement—we must use our leisure time more creatively than merely to fill it with diversions. And it is not only good for us, mentally and emotionally, to mingle socially valuable activities with those that are purely recreational, but best for us when we do so according to some sort of plan, some self-imposed schedule of requirements. Dr. Leslie S. Libow, chief of geriatric medicine at City Hospital Center in the Elmhurst section of New York City, reporting on an eleven-year study conducted by the National Institute of Mental Health, wrote that the most important of six hundred variable factors that keep some elderly people from succumbing to old age is the *organization* of daily behavior—their engaging in activities in a regulated and structured way, rather than haphazardly looking for things to do each day or just killing time. It puts us in mind of that old joke about the little girl in a very progressive, unprogramed school who petulantly said to her teacher, "Please, do I *have* to do whatever I *want* to do again all day?" It's no easier or more satisfying for a middle-aged or retired person to fill all his leisure with unplanned spontaneous fun than it is for a child. That's why becoming involved in an organized or at least planned series of activities that are important to us, some or even all of which are new, and not part of our previous life-style, is what we mean by rehearsal for retirement.

When we first arrive at middle age, retirement is many years away. Nonetheless, even in early middle age there is enough new leisure to begin to make a second life. And now that there is time, the possibilities are manifold; virtually anything you ever wanted to do—aside from things that absolutely require youth, such as making the Major Leagues or trying out for Miss America—are within reach. Granted, you can't start to study the violin at 45 and expect to perform in Symphony Hall, but you may certainly learn to play well enough to get immense pleasure from it. And granted, you can't begin to study Spanish at 45 and hope to pass for a native on your next trip to Spain, but you can learn enough in a year's time to chat with the natives of any remote Spanish village and gain infinitely more from your trip than you would have had you been restricted to English.

Do you doubt this? Do we hear you say that you can't teach an old dog new tricks? Wrong; definitely not so. Well, actually, we haven't any scientific data at hand about old dogs—but we do have about middle-aged human beings. A whole series of studies reported in *Aging and Society* show that, contrary to popular opinion, there is no decline in I.Q., and none in most kinds of learning ability, during the years of "full maturity," as middle age is sometimes called. We've all heard that brain weight decreases throughout life, and that each day a large number of brain cells die, never to be replaced. Scary stuff, that. But the fact is that you have ten billion of those cells to begin with and you can go through a long lifetime without even beginning to run short. It has been estimated that as few as 10 per cent of our brain cells disappear even over a long lifetime.

It is only the *fear* that you are too old to learn new tricks that limits you, and not any shortage of cerebral capacity.

Dr. Kenneth Soddy, former scientific director of the World Federation for Mental Health, reviewed the evidence concerning learning abilities a few years ago and concluded, in *Men in Middle Life*, that when it comes to learning new languages, playing musical instruments, painting, writing, and the like, the common belief that the middle-aged are too old to learn or that they learn new things more slowly is "on the whole, untrue . . . [but] may go a long way to create the condition to which it refers." Given equal time and motivation you can do just about as well at any of these things as a child—unless you think you can't.

And the notion that general intelligence diminishes throughout life is based on a common but erroneous way of studying aging. In a number of I.Q. studies made in the earlier decades of this century, older groups of people were tested and compared with younger groups; the older people showed lower scores than the younger people, from which it was concluded that I.Q. wanes during middle age. But these results are misleading, because they don't deal with the *same* people. I.Q. scores are significantly increased by education (they wouldn't be if they measured "pure" intelligence, but no widely used test really does that), and the older groups of people in these cross-section studies had, by and large, had less education than the younger groups, and for that reason, rather than their age, had lower scores. But in more recently conducted longitudinal studies which follow the same individuals over the years, not only is there no evidence of any decline in I.Q. before age 60, there even appear to be actual increases in some areas of I.Q., notably concept mastery. In one study cited by Dr. Riley, for instance, a group of college freshmen were tested with the Army Alpha intelligence test, and forty-two years later those who were still alive were given the same test—and showed an overall increase in scores. Even though longitudinal studies do show some I.Q. decline after age 60, it is much smaller in size than the seeming declines shown by cross-section studies. And recently, psychologist K. Warner Schaie of the University of Southern California completed a major longitudinal study which showed that distinct increases take place in various dimensions of intelligence during middle age and even old age.

The importance of the longitudinal (as opposed to the cross-sectional) approach to the study of middle age can hardly be overstressed. Dr. Riley points out that not only in the case of I.Q. but in income studies, and many other studies related to aging, researchers have often made the mistake of "erroneously inferring that differences among age categories in the society are *due* to the aging of the individuals," when, in fact, they are due to changes in the social milieu in which those groups of individuals grew up. To take an absurd example: older groups have fewer years of education than younger groups—but clearly, people don't lose the number of years of schooling they had as they grow older. The same is true of ability to learn, I.Q., earning capacity, many aspects of health, productivity on the job, and so on: according to studies made a generation ago older people are worse off than younger ones—but that is because they were worse off when they were young. Today's middle-aged people were more advantaged in their youth and will remain so.

The middle-aged person, then, can undertake many new ventures, can learn and master new skills of many sorts as well as ever. We two—the authors of this book—have recently begun to study piano, and take immense pleasure in our modest achievements. Right now we're playing fairly simple music, but we joke about being able to spend our long winter evenings, by the time we're 87, playing late Beethoven quartets arranged for four hands. We joke, but who knows? It may take that long, but perhaps we'll really do it.

That's our own particular thing, and it excites and delights us. Other people might prefer to read the classics they missed, or study cabinetmaking, or buy a telescope and learn astronomy, or become opera or ballet buffs, or learn to grow better and more delicious vegetables than they can buy in any store. Such new skills and activities enrich life far more than golf, tennis, and card games, in our opinion (though there's nothing wrong with those, either, if they're not the only leisure activities); they add stock to one's own corporation, the kind of stock that becomes true wealth.

And that's only the beginning of the possible. One can study for, and enter a new profession—one long desired but hitherto out of reach.

Our friend, Sidney L., a successful real-estate broker who is in his mid-50's, made a rather large amount of money in recent years; his wife, moreover, earns a good salary as a social worker and their children are now on their own. The law—especially the field of civil rights—has always fascinated Sidney, but he had never been anything more than a spectator; gradually, in recent years, it dawned on him that he could be more than that. So he gave up his business a year ago, and set out to fulfill his dream: he enrolled in law school.

At first it was terribly difficult because his study habits were rusty, and because he found it hard to cram far into the night like the younger students. But he did reasonably well in the first year anyway, and is finding the second one much easier.

Sidney's is by no means an isolated case. So many mature people have begun to go to college, or have returned to it in recent years, that a number of institutions have established special programs for adults minimizing their problems by tailoring courses and classes to their special needs. This started in a relatively small number of schools a few decades ago, chiefly with the aim of training or retraining women whose children had grown up and who wanted to go to work. The movement gathered strength and numbers during the 1960's as a result of the women's movement; more recently, such programs have broadened and begun to include middle-aged men who want to start a new career, or merely to enrich their lives. We are not referring to noncredit extension courses, but to solid programs aimed at degrees. The Adult Collegiate Education program at Queens College of the City University of New York, for instance, had an enrollment of 1600 adults seeking degrees, in May 1973. In the ten years of the program's existence, more than 80 per cent of the enrollees *have* earned degrees, and about 70 per cent of them have gone on to graduate school. One woman recently got her Ph.D. at the age of 71, after which she dyed her hair, lied about her age, and got a job.

When Dean Ernest Schwarcz, director of the program at Queens College, was asked why so many adults are taking college courses now, he listed several reasons, including increased leisure, the search for a higher income—and most interstingly, the goal of "creative early retirement." The phrase "creative early retirement" is an interesting one: it makes the important point that one can retire from the work he or she has been doing without retiring from personal growth or meaningful activities—or even from work.

Many people are forced into early retirements they don't want, and into leisure that hangs heavy around their necks; others stick too long with jobs or careers that bring them little satisfaction because, even though they no longer have children to support, they are afraid to try something new. But middle age—or at least postparental middle age—is the perfect time to make the bold move. A new career—prepared for by on-the-job training or by a stint in college—can enable such people to spend the second half of their adult lives doing something they really want to do, something that renews and reawakens them, fulfills old dreams (or brand-new ones), makes them feel young again and excited about life. A doctor we know, who was in general practice, had always wanted to be a psychiatrist. At 46, after months of searching talks with his wife and teen-age daughters, he gave up his practice, went back into the classroom, and spent several grueling years as student, intern, and resident. Then he passed his boards and has been a practicing psychiatrist ever since—and a more deeply satisfied man we have never known.

For the great bulk of us who have already had as much formal education as we want, or who have no hankering for a new career, there are many other ways to make a second life, using our new leisure time to pursue activities that are engrossing and satisfying in themselves and, by way of extra reward, are investments for our future.

One of the most important—and readily available—kinds of activity is increased involvement in the community and its organizations. During the parental years, most of our participation in community matters were centered around child-related groups —the schools, P.T.A., cooperative day-care centers, scouting, sports, and so on. When the need for such involvements is over, it can be highly rewarding to turn to other forms of community work. *Doubly* rewarding—for by so doing we serve both others and ourselves; we do work of which we are proud, and at the same time we reap very personal benefits. Many community organizations not only perform genuinely valuable functions and meet real community needs but provide a sound nucleus for making new friends, and an organized basis for social interaction. Just as important, the status one achieves as an active participant in such a group is a good replacement for the career status one is preparing to relinquish in the near future.

One elderly man in our town started taking up the slack in his life long ago, many years before retirement, by becoming an active member of the board of directors of Guild Hall, our local cultural center, where art exhibits, plays, and concerts are presented; it became one of the most important things in his life after his retirement. Another man took an interest in the school budget, although his own children were beyond the school years; he attended every Town Board meeting when the budget was under discussion, challenged any unsound assumption with facts he had culled from the annual reports of other school systems in the area, and became the most vocal advocate in the community of the elimination of boondoggling and valueless practices that waste our tax money.

In a New England community, we met and were told a good deal about one elderly man who, years earlier, when the pressure of the parental period was over, became both a leading figure in a local conservation society and an officer of his church. In recent years he has been performing a number of valuable services for his fellow members in both organizations, is highly respected by all who know him, and enjoys the demands both positions make on him. This has been particularly true since his retirement a few years ago: because of his many duties, he is never at a loss for something to do—and even more important, he knows that he is needed and that what he is doing is important. How wise this man was to establish important contacts with common-interest groups when his children were leaving school; how foresighted he was to plant roots in the community in time for them to grow deep, and to nourish his late middle life.

Some people, of course, loathe meetings and discussions, and therefore shun community organizations altogether. They are right to avoid the meetings and discussions—but they needn't remain cut off from important involvements in community life. They may, for instance, do well at more intimate and personal activities that are service-oriented, such as volunteer work in a hospital, reading to the blind, teaching English to the foreign-born, serving as adjunct teachers in remedial reading programs, and running thrift shops and used-book sales for local charities. There are innumerable opportunities of this kind; anyone who has the interest and the drive need only search out exactly the right ones.

Whatever you do with the extra free time the postparental years bring you, you will undoubtedly find that in addition, you and your spouse have a good deal more time together than you have had for a very long while. The survey by Dr. Leland J. Axelson mentioned earlier in this chapter showed that in the postparental years, substantial percentages of husbands and wives reported increased activities with their spouses—and increased "satisfaction with marital adjustment." That isn't a coincidence. The increase in shared activity could be the cause of the greater marital satisfaction—or the greater satisfaction could lead to the increase in shared activities. Whichever is the case, both the greater marital satisfaction and the increase in shared activities are related to—and, we are willing to bet, the results of—the extra money available and, to an even greater degree, the extra time. And it's not only a matter of quantity, but of quality; not just of more hours a day but of private and intimate time; time together, alone; time to be two people in that close, sharing, and marvelously united way that is possible only when there are no others constantly present.

All of which is a rather formal way of saying that for many people, the new freedom of middle age brings a resurgence, a deepening, a revitalization of love. For others, it does just the opposite, and with good reason. But this, as we said earlier, is another whole subject, one we'll take up in the next chapter.

3 *The Liberated Couple*

MID-LIFE AS THE TIME WHEN
HUSBAND AND WIFE CAN BE CLOSEST
AND MOST LOVING

For centuries, the poets have told us that love is for the young and fair; most of us have accepted as gospel the belief that as the years pass, the love of husband and wife wanes and, by middle age, is replaced by boredom, indifference, resignation, or bitterness, and often the need to escape. Fortunately, in the New Middle Age this is far from inevitable; indeed, for many the very opposite is true.

To give the poets their due, nothing *is* so wondrous as the first joys of new-found young love, the initial taste of pure ecstasy, the exquisite pleasure of learning that the beloved loves in return, the first tremulous exchange of kisses, touches, sentiments, and vows. But what happens to most young lovers after they have been married for twenty or thirty years is surprisingly different from the depressing scenarios that have been written for middle-aged couples throughout history; what once was fact is fact no longer.

The evidence of several recent research studies shows that, in general, postparental husbands and wives are more satisfied with their marriages than they were at any time during the long parental phase of married life. And it is our belief that even this fortunate majority has only begun to realize the new potential of married love in middle age.

That new potential has been created by a combination of circumstances all of which liberate the middle-aged man and woman to love and enjoy each other as they did in their first months together, and to be more complete together than ever within the marriage. First, the new climate of equal rights and obligations of both partners frees the couple much sooner, or even throughout marriage, from the conflicts and resentments created by the role specialization of the parental years—the partial or total relegation of the wife to child-care and household drudgery, the imposition on the husband of most or all of the burden of financial responsibility. Second, as the children reach maturity, the parents, at a relatively early time of life, are freed of the heavy responsibilities of the parental phase of their lives; more than that, the departure of the children from the home liberates the couple from the constant presence of others and from the constant demands of those others on their time and attention. As deeply gratifying as the parental phase was, in the postparental phase husband and wife have time and privacy, such as they have not had in many years, to rediscover the pleasures of being a marital twosome.

We read and hear a great deal about the shortcomings of one-to-one marital intimacy and the obsolescence of monogamous marriage. Critics of the old institutions range from avant-garde sociologists to militant feminists, and from liberal theologians to sexual libertarians; they say that under modern conditions a single monogamous relationship is too confining and too limited to meet all of the sexual, emotional, and intellectual needs of individuals over a lifetime. The critics are, in the main, undoubtedly right. One would think then, that by middle age the discontents of monogamous marriage would have reached critical mass and the marriage would be at a breaking point.

But not many middle-aged marriages *are* at a breaking point—because the breaking point comes much earlier. It is in young marriages that critical mass is reached, not old ones. Almost a third of all marriages that end in divorce do so within the first three years of marriage, and the median duration of all marriages ending in divorce is 6.9 years. It is during the first decade of marriage that six tenths of all divorces occur and during the first two decades that extramarital involvements are most common. A mere 3 per cent of all marital breakups take place after twenty-nine years of marriage. Married couples who reach the postparental years intact, or who remarry after divorce or widowhood, are relatively stable and far less likely than younger people to divorce again or to have outside relationships. For now, in postparental mid-life, the monogamous marriage really works; the factors that make it inadequate for so many younger couples have ceased to be relevant.

The cynic may reply that the middle-aged no longer care about romance or have merely given up, but contemporary research yields a more heartening answer: the evidence clearly shows that in middle age, there is a distinct increase in husband-wife companionship, equality, mutuality of interests, and understanding. As a result, both partners experience more overall satisfaction in the marriage.

These were the findings in the relatively small-scale study by Dr. Leland Axelson referred to in Chapter 2, but they are impressively reinforced by data from other studies that demonstrate that no matter how fervently couples may want children, and no matter how much they love and enjoy their children when they arrive, children change the marriage dramatically—and things can never be the same again until the children grow up.

Sociologist Jessie Bernard, writing in *The Future of Marriage* (1972), says about the advent of the first child, "The effect may be traumatizing. There is a drop in the indexes of marital satisfaction. Diverging interests—the wife's in her maternal and household responsibilities, the husband's in his professional career—can produce a drop in daily companionship. The marital interaction pattern seems to be muted." Dr. Bernard goes on to describe the school years of the children as the nadir of the marriage, with positive companionship at its lowest level. When the children reach their teens, the marriage may be devastated. But when the last child exits (and most do at about 18), *if* the woman has retained her larger role as a wife, in spite of everything, and not allowed herself to become only a mother, this segment of the marriage can be the best of all. Dr. Bernard comments, "This postparental stage of marriage is a brand-new phenomenon in human history. People did not live long enough in the past to reach it. . . . We are only now beginning to recognize the importance of this wholly new form of marriage; its potentials for happiness have hardly been explored." Dr. Bernard is talking about what we call the liberated couple.

The scientific evidence shows us the direction in which things are going, but it does not show us the limits to which they can go;

marital love and deeply rewarding companionship are at a new high level for many of the middle-aged, but, we feel, will reach even greater heights in the future.

To understand why we view this as likely—indeed, inevitable —look backward briefly with us to see how the modern concept of married love came into being. For it is something new under the sun, very special, and quite recent. One can scarcely find anything like it during the past 2500 years.

Sexual passion, has, to be sure, always existed—but hardly ever in combination with intellectual and emotional partnership. A man ate with his wife and slept with her, but for friendship and understanding consorted with other men.

Romantic love, too, has long existed—but not, until relatively recently, as part of marriage and daily life. Gentlemen in ancient Greece, upper-class men and women of imperial Rome, medieval lords and ladies of France and Italy, had the leisure and the social skills to make love an important part of their lives—but for them it was an extramarital game, an illicit diversion, rather than a part of married reality; the object of courtly love was always someone else's husband or wife, or an unmarried person, but definitely not one's own spouse.

Conjugal affection has often existed, especially among the moralistic middle classes who had neither time nor taste for love outside marriage—but only rarely did such affection involve companionship, mutual understanding, or the friendship of equals. Men adored women but viewed them as either angels or inferiors (and ruled them sternly); women loved men but viewed them as masters (and contrived to get around their iron rule). Tennyson summed up the Victorian male's image of the ideal wife:

> Her faith is fixt and cannot move,
> > She darkly feels him great and wise,
> > She dwells on him with faithful eyes,
> "I cannot understand; I love."

A few visionaries imagined a kind of married love which would include companionship and total intimacy—the seventeenth-century poet John Milton, for one, proclaimed that "in God's intention a meet and happy conversation is the chiefest and noblest end of marriage"—but this dream could not become a reality while men were dominant and women subordinate, for the imbalance of power created an impassable intellectual and emotional gulf between them. Male dominance was basically the result of the need for specialization: the man's greater strength made him the better candidate for heavy work and defense, while the woman's lactating breast and lesser strength made her the better candidate for infant care and homemaking. Equality, sharing, and companionship could become part of married love only when men and women were emancipated from the need to play very different roles throughout life.

And that emancipation did begin to take place gradually as technology and industrialization made it less essential for the woman to spend her life preparing food and sewing clothing, and made the man's greater physical strength less and less significant.

Among the innovations included in emancipation—most of them resisted, some welcomed, by men—were higher education and legal rights for women, the free choice of marital partner by the young, the entry of women into the labor force, and the liberalization of divorce laws. Women became less dependent upon men, more like them in intellectual capacity, less servantlike, less self-doubting, devious, and timid; and marriage became ever less a strictly practical and productive institution and ever more a heterosexual companionship.

Or at least that's how things seemed to be going in the 1920's and 1930's. But the evolutionary road wasn't a smooth one. Men did not give up all their privileges easily—and women, still powerfully molded by cultural tradition, continued to envision their major identity as made up of the roles of homemaker and mother. So even though girls went to the same schools as boys, grew up to have the same legal rights and the vote, and were often trained for skilled work in the outside world, most married women still retreated into domesticity after a brief period of childlessness and remained there throughout their adult lives. But even though they had chosen the domestic role, it became a major source of marital discontent for them; having sighted broader horizons, women found housekeeping confining and demeaning. They suffered from what was known in the 1950's and 1960's as the "trapped-housewife syndrome," resented their husbands' freedom, grew hostile. Worse still, when the wife turned to full-time mothering and homemaking, and the husband became the sole wage earner of the family, the pair drifted into a partial resumption of the traditional master-servant relationship and thereby lost much of what had been best about companionship-love.

Although Betty Friedan, Kate Millett, and Germaine Greer have pictured the male oppressors as happy with this situation, the truth is that many married men with children felt that something was missing from their lives. They had liked the intimacy and the understanding they and their wives had shared when they were childless and more nearly equals. Many such a man, after parenthood had changed things, found himself longing for a woman who really understood him, and who could talk his language, appreciate his triumphs, sympathize with his concerns—and tell him hers. No wonder his secretary or some female colleague began to look so attractive to him; he felt sexually drawn to her, but often what underlay that pull was the yearning for someone to talk to.

This, then, was the dilemma: many men found marriage disappointing, less rewarding than they expected it to be—and as for women, discontent was rampant in kitchens and nurseries throughout the land. But hardly anyone told. Hardly anyone dared. Motherhood was sacred and was woman's highest calling; a woman who disagreed felt guilty and kept her nasty secret to herself. Homemaking was supposed to be creative and important, and all of the women's magazines assured her that it was a fact. And so the farce continued.

Roles were so rigid that any deviation from them was always good for a laugh. It was a standard cartoon, movie, or television joke to show a totally disheveled man in a ruffled apron burning the peas or trying desperately to clean up the filthy kitchen before his wife came home from visiting her sick mother and had hysterics. It was supposed to be equally comical to see the helpless young wife teeter precariously on the edge of a stepladder trying to change a light bulb, or valiantly attempt to fix Junior's toy by hammering in a screw.

Even more ludicrous, from the fixed-role viewpoint, was the woman with a career; she was invariably portrayed as sexless, tough-talking, and terribly plain—but we all knew that as soon as the Right Guy came along, she would take off her glasses and be beautiful, turn mushy and feminine, buy sheer negligees for her trousseau, and cheerfully abandon her career. Almost all of us, women as well as men, found it wonderfully reassuring to be told that the career woman was a freak of nature, or that within her formidable exterior there was a purring kitten, just waiting to be let out.

The sharp differences in our conceptions of men and women, and the resulting differences in the status and activities of husbands and wives, perpetuated the gulf between the sexes. It was particularly apparent at married-couples parties—and surely you remember what they used to be like. After a few general greetings and a small amount of semiflirtatious cross talk, the "girls" inevitably assembled on one side of the room to talk about the local pediatrician, what was happening at school, a new recipe for quiche, the scarcity of dressmakers, how to start begonias from slips, gynecologists, the difficulty of getting grass stains out of tennis shorts, the thirteen-year-old bully who had just moved into the neighborhood, and whose blue sports car was parked behind the hedge around the corner from Sally Bennett's house several afternoons a week.

It wasn't that these women had limited mental capacities; some of them were college graduates, some had worked at interesting jobs, and not so long ago they had all been interested in all kinds of things. But in those days, a woman chose either a career *or* marriage, and since it was moderately deviant to choose a career instead of marriage, the great bulk of women found themselves with lives so cluttered up with the business of running a house and family that they had no time for the variety of other pursuits that would have kept them from feeling inferior and trapped.

Meanwhile, what were the husbands doing at those parties? They were talking to each other about the state of the stock market, the situation in the latest trouble spot of the world, the upcoming World Series, taxes, unions, and who was likely to get the nomination at the convention. Twentieth-century men didn't retire to the library for brandy and a cigar as Victorian gentlemen used to do—but they retired, all the same, from mixed-sex conversation into their own comfortable all-male camaraderie.

The failure of communications between the sexes was not limited to parties, but existed in the home as well. Conversation, which had been so vital and exciting to the man and woman when they were single or newly married, now was commonly restricted to such mundane matters as the management of the home and children, discussion of planned purchases, or odds and ends of news about friends and relatives. It was not customary for men to discuss their work or their worldly concerns with women, although many wives would have welcomed such sharing.

The longer they were married, the more limited the wives became in intellectual outlook, the more the husbands became encapsulated in their own world—and the poorer the quality of communication between them became.

As David L. Cohn, a popular social critic of the time, said in his 1943 book *Love in America: An Informal Study of Manners and Morals in American Marriage:*

> It is the rare husband and wife who pull up the chairs and spend an hour talking for their own pleasure about non-utilitarian things. The husband has his business, the wife her "cultural interest," and never the twain shall meet. Their intellectual and spiritual lives remain personal and separate, with the result that while their marriage is a physical union and an economic organization it involves no spiritual communion and no completion of minds. This is a large factor in the loneliness of people and their all-too-common feeling of frustration in marriage.

How could it have been otherwise? One would hardly expect a bachelor electrical engineer, say, and the maid who cleaned his apartment to sustain an ongoing stimulating dialogue; and the married engineer and the woman who ran the household—if they had no areas of common interest or close companionship—were not likely to do much better.

But what about the rare wife who did have a real profession or career, and whose daily life and intellectual interests paralleled those of her husband? If she was childless, the situation was, indeed, likely to be one of relative equality and to involve a high level of continuing companionship. However, if she tried to combine work with motherhood, she usually wound up doing double duty; she had to handle all of the woman's traditional roles as well as the new ones, and this left her no time for marital companionship—but plenty for resentment. The situation was known to be so difficult that virtually no one opted for it.

The typical working wife-and-mother in the 1940's—and in fact, right up to very recent years—rushed frantically from her office at closing time to do some shopping on her way home. The day-care center being unknown, it was her mother or a neighbor, the maid or mother's helper who had held things together in some fashion during the day—but the moment the working mother arrived home she was assaulted by the whole array of problems; there were fights among the children, the daily collection of runny noses or bruises, missing buttons, homework problems—and while she tried to deal with all this, she had to find time to wash her face, fix her hair, get the dinner under way, and welcome her husband home. After dinner, she did the dishes (usually without help), got the children off to bed, and afterward had to look over the day's mail, write instructions for the next day's baby-sitter, return a few phone calls, perhaps do her nails. The evening was over before it began, without time for communion between husband and wife. It was little wonder that most men, although they liked the extra money their wives earned, objected to their working; even though they themselves were not the best of companions, they felt neglected and ignored by their wives.

It rarely occurred to these men—or if it did they generally rejected the thought—that they could solve the problem by sharing the homemaking and child-care duties. They had been culturally conditioned to think of such tasks as "woman's work," and took a perverse pride in being totally incompetent in those areas. Most interestingly, the overburdened wives had had exactly the same conditioning as their husbands and it rarely occurred to them (or, at least, seemed right to them) to ask for assistance. Everybody knew that a woman who let her husband wash dishes, except in a dire emergency, was a poor wife—and that a husband who did wash them was somehow not quite manly.

An old friend of one of us, Pat S., was a singer who occasionally did some church or concert work, or got a job in a minor-league musical. Her two children were the most spick-and-span in the neighborhood, and Pat was known as a compulsive housekeeper. If she worked at night, she did everything by day, and when she worked or rehearsed during the day, she stayed up late at night to finish her housework. Her explanation of why she drove herself to such limits was, "When I got married, I undertook to be a wife and mother, and I never forget that that's my first responsibility. I enjoy my work, but I don't want my family to be cheated in any way by what is, after all, my luxury."

That was less than twenty years ago, but today Pat's story sounds strangely archaic. For there has been a significant shift in the attitudes of young men and women concerning the woman's right to work during the busy parental years, and the sharing of household and child-care tasks. The women's movement has done a great deal to make the "shared-role" pattern of marriage seem acceptable to modern husbands and wives, and the traditional rigid role division seem archaic. As we saw earlier, more wives than ever work even during the child-rearing years, and thus share the husband's economic burden; similarly, more husbands play at least some part in homemaking tasks.

Ideally, according to some avant-garde thinkers, the sharing should be total: husband and wife should each work outside for half a week and run the home for the remainder. That Utopian vision remains impractical for people in conventional jobs; in addition, cultural tradition still wields a strong enough hand to prevent most young couples from making such a full-scale commitment to total sharing. For such reasons, sociologist Ira L. Reiss predicts that full-scale role-sharing is not likely to become common within the twentieth century.

What is becoming common—and may well be the prevailing

pattern before the end of the century—is the relatively complete sharing of roles during the childless period, and, when children arrive, a compromise between the traditional pattern and the shared-role pattern. Like all compromises, it's less than ideal, but it is undoubtedly an improvement over what used to be, not only for the woman but for the marital relationship—and hence for the husband—and therefore for the child.

Jeffrey and Susan K., people we know intimately, are in their upper twenties and have one child, two-year-old Amy. Susan used to work for an advertising agency but gave up her job in order to take care of her own child; it was a difficult decision to make, but after careful consideration, both young parents decided that they did not want their child to be reared by strangers during her most formative years. Susan does plan to go back to work when she can, after Amy and a planned second child are both in school.

In the meantime, she is completing her graduate studies at a nearby university. Jeffrey teaches and gets home by about four o'clock, so several days a week, as soon as he comes in, Susan rushes off to her classes; Jeffrey takes charge of Amy and the house and prepares the dinner. He also takes over at other times such as when Susan is busy with her little-theater group or involved in political activities.

But role flexibility doesn't work in just one direction to draw Jeffrey into what used to be "woman's work"; Susan, though she does not presently earn any money, has recently finished painting and papering the bedrooms and stripping and refinishing some old furniture. She does not see these jobs as "man's work" but rather as "people's work," and she happens to be very skillful at them. Often, Sue and Jeff work together on more difficult tasks, such as laying a ceramic tile floor or repairing the roof. Their mode of role utilization hasn't cut into their "meet and happy conversation"; they share all their daily experiences, read and talk about the same books, understand each other's minor triumphs and failures, care deeply about all of each other's thoughts and feelings.

Jeffrey and Susan's life-style represents a considerable liberation and a genuine advance toward the companionship ideal. All three members of the family benefit from it: Amy has the full experience of both a male and a female parent, Jeffrey has a companion in his wife, and Susan not only has a companion in her husband but feels much less confined and less gone-to-seed than the trapped housewife of ten or twenty years ago.

Yet while Susan and Jeffrey are far more liberated than their own parents were at their age, they are less liberated than their own parents are today; as admirable as Susan and Jeffrey's adaptation is, it still falls short of what is possible for the postparental middle-aged pair. Jeffrey is the sole earner, feels the burden of his responsibility—and, to a large extent, controls the purse strings; Susan, of course, shares in most decision-making about major purchases, but every now and then one glimpses her hidden resentment when she wants to buy a new dress or a piece of furniture that Jeffrey says they can't afford.

Lack of equality in regard to money is a flaw in liberation, for, to a large extent, money is power, and in the old days it was a prime source of marital discord. Until recently, it was taken for granted by everyone that it was the husband's job to support his wife—even if they were divorced. If he controlled the money, to a large degree he controlled her.

It is far more common today for couples to have joint bank accounts and to share the responsibility of spending as they share so many other things; this automatically does away with many of the old money squabbles that plagued so many marriages. But the money question is still least troublesome when the woman has an income.

Sociologists Robert O. Blood, Jr., and Donald M. Wolfe, in their 1960 study entitled *Husbands and Wives: The Dynamics of Married Living,* said that their survey showed money-earning work to be among the most potent sources of "marital power" (the degree to which a partner shares in or controls various important family decisions). At all social levels, they reported, working wives had more power than nonworking wives, and wives with full-time jobs had more power than wives with part-time jobs. Blood and Wolfe found that whatever the balance of power while the couple remained childless, it shifted toward the husband when the young mother gave up her job to care for her baby, ceased earning money, and was confined with relatively few opportunities to participate in recreational or organizational meetings. "Under these circumstances," they said, "parenthood brings a sudden loss of resources to the wife, combined with increased need for husbandly support. It is no wonder, therefore, that the wife's dependence increases." So, then, as a wife's dependence increases, the husband's power increases, equality becomes inequality, resentments grow, and companionship diminishes; by the time the children are teen-agers, love and affection may reach a low ebb.

But work provides women with much more than earnings and marital power; as we have said, it gives them a variety of outside contacts and ego satisfactions. Consequently, they generally have a relatively high level of mental health. Several studies cited by Professor Bernard show that women relegated to the role of housewife have higher rates of mental and emotional disorders than women who work, and that working women complain less often than do housewives of pains, ailments, or not feeling well enough to do the things they want to do.

No woman with children can liberate herself—and her marriage —from the hazards of inequality as easily as can the postparental woman. Initially, most of us thought of women's liberation as a youth movement, but the middle-aged are making the most of it. Far larger percentages of middle-aged women than younger ones are taking advantage of the newly "liberated" positions and salaries, and not only are their husbands sharing in the financial benefits but in the benefits of the wife's increased satisfaction and sense of ego fulfillment, for, as should be obvious, a happy person is a better companion than an unhappy one.

We are not trying to say that no marriage can be a happy one unless the wife works. But we *are* personally convinced by a wealth of data that, in general, working wives have better self-images and are happier than nonworking wives, although, of course, there are special circumstances that make for exceptions. In any case, even the nonworking wife is apt to experience a surge of egalitarianism within the marriage during the postparental period. The Blood and Wolfe study found that middle-aged wives exhibited more self-confidence, and shared more fully in marital decision-making, than younger wives. It is very likely that this is as true today as it was a decade and a half ago. Like Susan and Jeffrey, many young couples share a number of roles and have relatively egalitarian marriages —but try as they will, the presence of dependent children forces them into a significant degree of inequality. The ideal of a true peer partnership remains far more attainable for the postparental couple.

Bernice comments

Like everyone else in our age group, we have a number of friends who were divorced and who remarried in mid-life. In a few cases, the men married somewhat younger, childless women who almost immediately produced one or more babies. The babies are perfectly nice babies, and I'm sure the proud parents are very happy—but every time some close-to-40 mother and a 50-ish father tell us that they "haven't been anywhere in months because the baby's had one thing after another," or "it will probably be years before we ever get to Europe together because it's so hard to travel with little children," I must confess that I think these people mildly demented. All of those fathers have already raised one brood, and some are even grand-fathers. "How," I keep wondering, "can they do it all over again—and why? When are they going to stop being parents and just be with each other? They'll never have time." Then I realize, of course, that this is the only mode of married life they have ever known; they have no idea what it's like for us, and now, they'll never find out.

And that is the key to why I feel as I do, because life *is* very good for us; to give up our freedom and intimacy would be an act of sheer madness. I'm delighted that I had three children, and especially de-lighted that I had them all when I was in my twenties. As Ecclesiastes tells us, *To every thing there is a season, and a time to every purpose under the heaven.*

I raised my children during the season for raising children and it was good. But now I am at a time befitting to a different purpose—to do the work that fulfills my needs for creativity and for status—and to share my life with Morton, my equal partner, as we enjoy all of the pleasures and privileges available to any young, newly married couple.

For there is, as we said at the outset, another kind of liberation of the middle-aged couple—liberation from the intrusion upon their time, energy, and especially privacy, of other persons; liberation to become intimate again. The several studies we have already named have been in general agreement that, along with greater sharing of tasks and decision-making, the postparental stage of marriage brings increased companionship and general marital satisfaction to both partners. For one thing, it restores the time to talk to each other. A study made by a team of social scientists at Cornell University found that parents of young children or schoolchildren talk to each other only half as much as they did before the children arrived. It isn't just the lack of mutuality of interests that interferes, but the lack of the privacy that is essential to really intimate communication.

Morton comments

I remember it as if it were only yesterday. One small baby—and daily life instantly became a wholly different thing. There was always a sleep-in maid (my first wife, a performer, was often away rehearsing, or performing out of town), and even in the living room I felt that any conversation was apt to be overheard. Later, in addition to the omnipresent maid, there were playmates and schoolmates, new friends from the park (and their mothers or baby-sitters), old friends from camp (and *their* mothers or baby-sitters). And, of course, overnighting grandparents, cousins, and others. Sometimes the maid would go out for the night and sooner or later Jeff would go to sleep, but there was rarely a feeling of wholly safe privacy in which to be spontaneously and playfully sexual, or to vigorously and loudly air differences. Even the bedroom door is no barrier against the child awakened by voices, a nightmare, or a touch of colic.

I hasten to say that I never for an instant regretted having become a father; from the beginning, I accepted the fact that one gives up private-couple life when one has a child. And having a son added immeasurably to my life at that time, still does, and, I hope, always will. The changes that parenthood brought about were proper and fine—for that period of my life. And it was surely not the loss of privacy that led to the end of the marriage; there were other, far more fundamental, changes taking place in my wife and myself which, after a number of years, led us so far apart as to render the marriage emotionally invalid.

Had that not happened, privacy would eventually have returned. But it did happen, and now I am in another marriage altogether. And one that is doubly blessed—first, by the nature of the relationship between Bernice and me; and second, by the fact that our marriage possesses the middle-aged boon of privacy and intimacy. We continually luxuriate in that milieu, in our oneness, in our freedom as a couple. We love to visit friends and to go to parties, but relish coming home afterward to our own quiet retreat. We love having friends, and our various children, stay overnight and spend a weekend with us, but while they are here we often *miss* each other; sometimes, after they have been here for a couple of days, each of us feels—well, there is no way to put it but *lonely for each other*. When our guests leave, we are genuinely sorry to see them go—but then we turn to each other and feel complete again.

For a minority of couples, the transition to the postparental years works out very differently; it may result in a sudden deterioration of the marriage. These are the couples who were so engrossed in the partnership of raising a family that they had not realized how little else they had in common. Alone with each other again, their liberation and privacy leads not to renewed companionship and intimacy, but to feelings of imprisonment, boredom, irritation, and the particularly poignant loneliness that comes of being isolated with someone in a loveless relationship. These are the people who totally startle their unsuspecting friends by getting a divorce in middle age, without any advance warnings. The following case is typical:

Grace and John M. had always seemed to have run-of-the-mill problems typical of their time in life: money problems in the early years; teen-age problems later on when one of the children was discovered to be using drugs; a certain amount of recurring conflict about Grace's part-time job and her larger career aspirations. But by and large they presented a solid front and seemed to have a gracious way of life; their many friends thought of them as a happily married, if occasionally harried, couple.

Then the children left. At first, things looked better than ever: with extra money and time, Grace and John finally began to make plans to realize their long-time dream of building a country house and leaving the city behind. During the next two years, they seemed busy, happy, excited, and deeply involved in the planning, building, and furnishing of their house. Finally, the last bedspread was selected, the last painting hung, and they moved in. Two weeks later, Grace packed her bags, took a cab to the train station, and headed for New York; she checked into a hotel and, before she even unpacked her bags, contacted a divorce lawyer.

All of Grace and John's friends were shocked; there had been no clues—or none that we had been able to see, no hints of infidelity, some awful wrong, or any long-standing grievance that had never been resolved. What had happened was not uncommon: left alone together, without the children and the stimulation of the city, Grace and John had nothing to say to each other, and even worse than that, they seemed constantly to get on each other's nerves. Neither one could make a move that wasn't irritating to the other.

As Grace told us much later, she and John had never been particularly happy with each other, but they had not come to grips with the problem. At first, they hadn't even been aware of the emptiness of their relationship because they were so distracted by problems of mere survival with very little money and two children to raise. Later, they were both absorbed by and held together by their severe problems with the older child; in addition, their warm interaction with friends and families in the neighborhood kept them socially busy and cheerful most of the time. They weren't even aware of how little time they ever spent alone together.

When the children grew up and left, and a great silence descended upon them, it was much more agreeable to throw themselves into the dream-house project than to face the truth. For two years, they worked side by side solving the problems of the house —but when the house was finished, they were out of business. They finally saw the sad truth—that they could collaborate only on external problems, but could never begin to solve the internal ones of their marital relationship, which was without any emotional or intellectual validity, and no longer had any reason for being. And therefore ended.

Most of us feel deeply sorry for those few friends whose marriages break up in middle age. But for many of them, divorce is the only way to salvage the Prime Time of their lives from ruin. For while middle age can be a lengthy, joyous, liberated, fulfilling, and intensely pleasurable period of life, it is not likely to be any of those things (except lengthy) if spent in the imprisonment of an outworn, outgrown, and loveless marriage. Divorce can be the greatest liberation of all for those who really need it.

The question is, who really needs it? Only those who have given their marriage time to recover, by itself, from the strains and stresses of the parental years, or who have exhausted the possibilities of reviving or rebuilding it with professional help. For with the easing of family pressures and financial demands, and the regaining of privacy, many a marriage that seems dull, worn, and distant improves spontaneously. Even of those that are too badly eroded or torn by conflict to do so, at least a minority can be improved through the aid of marriage counselors or therapists. Unless the match was a bad one to begin with (as was the case with Grace and John) or the process of deterioration has gone very far, the original basis of mutual attraction may still exist and be capable of revitalization.

But even where a sound original basis still exists, it may take much hard work to rediscover it and to find out what has gone wrong. A woman we interviewed told us how astonished she was to discover, when she began psychotherapy, that over the years, she had allowed herself to become totally child-oriented. She had given less and less time and attention to her husband and become aware of it only when she noticed that she was getting nothing in return. With the children gone, she was able to pay attention to her mate again and found that she really liked him—and that he was highly responsive to her attention.

Similarly, a man we interviewed had drifted away from his wife and into excessive absorption in his work, urban planning. Over the years, he had come to spend more and more of his evenings, and sometimes even his weekends, with his partner and his fellow professionals; his work was challenging, absorbing, difficult, and he liked doing nothing better than to be with people who understood and shared his enthusiasms and his difficulties. In the early years, he had made some effort to discuss his work with his wife, but as it grew ever more complex he didn't bother any more.

When the children went off to college, his wife was left with a vacuum in her life; she had neither any meaningful duties at home nor any companionship with her husband. The marriage soon became turbulent and unstable, and the couple sought joint counseling. As the problems became clear, the counselor suggested that the husband might offer his wife a part-time job in his office. He did, she accepted, and within a short time she was not only delighted and intrigued with her new career but was soon dipping into her husband's library on urban planning. He was extremely pleased by her interest and her growing knowledge, and enjoyed being able to talk over his current difficulties and achievements with her at any time of the day or night. In the past three years, their marriage has become close-knit and warm, and both partners feel that they are enjoying life more than they have in a very long while.

We heard this kind of story many times—with myriad variations, of course—from our other interviewees. Many a marriage enjoys a renascence in middle age, for the conjoined, shared, intimate relationship gratifies the deepest needs and fully expresses the capacities of the liberated couple. It is not only the sole mode of living that satisfies the requirements of most mature people, but it is the kind of marriage that really works in the Prime Time of life.

4 Passionate Middle Age

THE DRAMATIC CHANGE TAKING PLACE
IN THE SEX LIFE OF MIDDLE AGE

Not long ago, Jill and Norman D. turned down a dinner invitation because they wanted to spend a long evening alone together at home dining leisurely with music, good wine, good talk, and then slowly and luxuriously making love in front of a crackling fire and, perhaps, again later on in bed. Which hardly sounds extraordinary except that they are in their late forties and have been married for many years.

Jill and Norman—among the best exemplars of the Prime Time way of life we have met—needed that evening with each other because they had just been through one of those much-too-busy periods we are all familiar with. For three days they'd had house guests. Then the next two evenings had been preempted by business and organizational meetings for both of them; and right after that, Norman had had to go out of town for four days. On the long-distance phone, he and Jill had promised each other that no matter what came along, they would accept no invitations for his first evening back but would stay home and catch up with each other about everything they had been doing and thinking, enjoy a bottle of the new Beaujolais that had just arrived, and, most important of all, take plenty of time for the warm, loving, physical contact that is as essential a part of their relationship today as ever in the past.

Naturally, they did not explain any of this to their would-be hostess but simply said they were busy that evening. For one thing, Jill and Norman have a normal sense of privacy; for another, if they *had* told the truth, their friend—a much younger woman—would have been incredulous or even mildly scandalized. It is a rare young person who has any idea of the importance and the power that sexual passion still retains for many of the middle-aged, or who can, without acute discomfort, envision people nearly the age of his or her own parents performing sexual acts at all, let alone with tenderness and ferocity, playfulness and lust.

It is true, of course, that by middle age most people used to find the fires of sexual passion dying down if not threatening to go out altogether; characteristically, beyond the age of forty, marital coitus was infrequent, perfunctory, and joyless. But in recent decades, and especially within the past generation, a major change has been taking place in this pattern: clinical researchers have discovered that physiologically, the capacity for sexual activity in middle age is far greater than it had been thought to be; effective treatments for many common middle-age sexual difficulties have been found; and the latest national survey has shown that, thanks to a generally changing outlook on sexuality, the average frequency and the variety of sexual activities of the middle-aged have increased sharply. While the uninformed still cling to outmoded attitudes, for those who have discovered the New Middle Age sexual passion has assumed an importance and legitimacy it has not had for many centuries—if ever.

The change runs counter to a tradition that goes back even further than Christianity. " 'Tis unseemly for the old man to love," Ovid wrote nearly two thousand years ago, and Roman satirists often made fun of the lecherous middle-aged man and hot-blooded middle-aged woman. But Christianity turned mere scorn into condemnation, for when it became part of Church dogma that sex was justified only by procreation, sexual activity beyond the fertile years could only be viewed as sinful. The attitudes associated with this doctrine became deeply entrenched in the culture; even when Protestantism moderated the official position of a large part of the Christian world, the belief remained general that after the years of youth, sexual activity was, at best, ridiculous, and at worst, unnatural. Less than a century ago, the great authority on sex, Richard von Krafft-Ebing, viewed sex in older people with deep suspicion, asserting, for instance, that sexual desire in an older man "may be the precursor of senile dementia" and an early indication of on-coming "intellectual weakness."

The moral disapproval of sex for the middle-aged and the eld-erly often assumed the disguise of folk wisdom passed down from generation to generation. A few items of that "wisdom":

—There is just so much sexuality in a lifetime; if one squanders it in youth, he will have none left by middle age.

—After the menopause, women feel little or no sexual desire; such desire is a sign of abnormality or perversion.

—In middle age it is normal for men to lose their sexual powers; during the 40's—and certainly no later than the 50's—many men have to accept impotence as a fact of life.

—Actually, impotence at this time isn't really so bad, because middle-aged men, like middle-aged women, don't really miss sex. They feel no desire, and anyway, they care more about other things.

In relatively recent times, with the advent of modern surgery, two more pieces of folk wisdom joined the list:

—After a hysterectomy at any age, a woman no longer feels sexual desire nor receives any pleasure from intercourse.

—After a prostatectomy, a man is permanently impotent.

There was just enough plausibility to some of these myths to make people go on believing them even when research proved them generally false. It is a fact, for example, that until relatively recently many older women did, indeed, have physical problems that interfered with sexual pleasure.

For one thing, before the days of modern obstetrical care, a woman who had had several babies—or even one large one—was apt to have a badly stretched vagina and weakened pelvic musculature, with the result that much of the sensation of coital contact essential to both her own pleasure and her husband's was missing. Under these circumstances it was natural for the couple to reluctantly agree that "it was no longer meant to be" at their time of life.

Even more commonly, beyond menopause or upon removal of the ovaries, many a woman suffered from estrogen deficiency. The tissues of her vagina became thin and atrophic, and her production of lubricating fluid during sexual excitement diminished or even ceased; as a consequence of these changes, intercourse was harsh and painful, and resulted in severe itching, burning, and, sometimes, bleeding. Again, all this seemed proof positive that beyond menopause it was natural to give up sexual activity.

Men, too, had some realistic reasons for believing that middle age was the end, or at least the beginning of the end, of sexual life for them. What with the traditional Christian hostility to variations in sexual technique and to refinements in methods of arousal, and the sexual passivity considered proper for the "good" woman, it was no wonder that many a man grew sexually bored; being bored, felt little desire; feeling little desire, thought himself failing; and thinking himself failing, often failed. His wife's gynecological ailments and resulting disinclination to coitus served to reinforce the effect and to make him feel glumly certain that his sexual drive had reached its natural end. The process was often hastened when, during the middle years, at the height of both his career and his community activities, which took large quantities of time and energy, his stamina was noticeably dropping below its youthful levels; a man could be too tired at bedtime to be interested in sex, or interested but too tired to pursue the interest with the vigor he had formerly known.

The loss of vigor has always been alarming to men who do not understand that it is perfectly normal and not an omen of doom. Even before middle age, men often notice that their erections no longer arrive unbidden or almost immediately upon having any thought of sex or watching their wives undress; they may also notice that their erections are not as rigid as formerly, and sometimes weaken or even fade away during the sex act. Their orgasms come more slowly—which is fine, except that sometimes they find it difficult to achieve orgasm at all. Even if that never happens, it definitely takes longer after an orgasm before the next one is possible—hours, perhaps, or even days. Such signs, apparently bearing out the gloomy predictions of tradition, make many a man apprehensive—which only serves to make things worse, since nothing so effectively counteracts the involuntary neuromuscular responses producing erection as anxiety. When a man fears that it's all up with him, it's all down with him; he has created a self-fulfilling prophecy.

Just how early these signs used to arrive, and how devastating they could be when interpreted in the light of the old tradition, one can judge from these blackly pessimistic lines penned by Byron:

> My days are in the yellow leaf;
>> The flowers and fruits of Love are gone;
> The worm, the canker, and the grief
>> Are mine alone!

These lines are from a poem entitled "On This Day I Complete My Thirty-sixth Year."

One other factor, growing out of our Western prudishness, played (and to some extent still plays) an important part in making our traditional prophecies about the failure of sex in middle age self-fulfilling. This is our deeply rooted custom of concealing from our children the fact that we, their parents, enjoy sex. Because many people, even today, keep this secret, children—no matter how old or sophisticated—are often unwilling or unable to see their parents as sexual beings. Nearly all children, when they first learn about coitus, stoutly deny that *their* parents would do such a thing, or at least that they do it *now*. Even later, they tend to minimize the part that sex plays in their parents' lives, a fact which has been verified by social scientists. At Brandeis University, for instance, two psychologists gave a group of students a sentence-completion test in which they were asked to complete the statement, "Sex for most old people. . . ." The students, whose ages ranged from 17 to 23, almost all filled in the blank with statements that ended with such words as "negligible," "unimportant," and "past." With such an attitude, young people run the risk, as they arrive at middle age, of seeing themselves approaching the end of their sexual lives, and of behaving as they long ago learned to believe they should behave when youth was gone. This study was made some years ago, and today, it is true, an increasing number of the parents of young children are conveying the truth to them; those children will reach their own middle age with a far more positive set of expectations of it than those whose parents concealed or played down the truth. But there are still too many of the latter.

All these factors had profoundly negative effects on middle-aged sexual behavior in the past and, because no cultural tradition is swiftly uprooted, still affect many of us to some extent, even now. The lucky ones recognize what the problem is and take steps to combat it; the unlucky ones do not, and lose the precious gift of sexuality decades before they need to. Ken and Harriet N., close friends of ours, are among the lucky ones. A few years ago when they learned that we had been interviewing people around the country for Morton's last book, *Sexual Behavior in the 1970s,* they felt impelled to tell us a story they thought we would find interesting. We did, but it belongs in this book, not that one, so here it is.

That year Ken and Harriet, who were in their early 40's, had rented a charming but tiny and frail old farmhouse in Connecticut for the summer. One night, during their first week of vacation, they were just becoming highly enthusiastic about their lovemaking when their 13-year-old daughter Nancy, in the adjoining bedroom, banged on the wall and called, "For Pete's sake, what're you doing in there? You're keeping me awake!" Needless to say, Ken and Harriet lost their enthusiasm at once; in fact, Ken also lost his erection and nothing they did would coax it back that night.

A couple of nights later, having warned each other not to make noise, they started to make love again, but the old, thin walls apparently conveyed every creak of the bed, and again, *in medias res,* Nancy banged on the wall and shouted that she wished they would "stop fixing things in the middle of the night." This time, the damage was more serious, for not only was Ken once more unable to resume, but this time felt overwhelmed by anxiety and the irrational conviction that he was getting old, that his manhood was failing, that it was all over with him as far as sex was concerned. Even when Nancy went to spend the night at her friend's house, Ken was so anxious about his ability to perform that although he started off well enough, he soon lost all interest, broke into a cold sweat, and became deeply depressed. Harriet, who had been all sympathy and warmth up to that point, suddenly took the matter as a reflection of Ken's feelings for her and grew angry and upset, which only made matters worse.

After two weeks of continuing difficulty, Ken and Harriet decided that the situation warranted a trip to the city to consult a marriage counselor. The problem proved to be far less profound than they had feared. They realized, when they examined the possibilities with the counselor, that Nancy could not have interrupted them through sheer ignorance, for she already knew about sex, nor through malice, for she was a sweet and loving child. What then? With only a little prompting it came to them, in a burst of recognition, that in all likelihood, although Nancy knew about sex, she had not actually associated the noises she heard with sexual activity because it would never occur to her that her parents still did such a "young" thing.

The real problem, the counselor suggested, lay not in what Nancy thought or believed, but in their own unconscious acceptance of the same tradition that had affected her—the feeling that middle-aged parents, people in their 40's who weren't going to have any more children, were—or should be—beyond all that. Ken and Harriet, having such feelings at an unconscious level, had been acutely embarrassed and ashamed at having been "caught" (as they perceived it) doing something unseemly and inappropriate, and Ken had unconsciously "solved" the problem by becoming so anxious that the sex act was no longer possible.

The difficulty was thus a cultural problem, not a neurotic one, and, once exposed, required relatively little further discussion. Harriet and Ken, vastly relieved, spent another hour with the counselor working out their feelings enough to be able to go home and discuss the matter openly with Nancy. She listened, astonished, and told them that she honestly thought they had been repairing some of the old furniture they had just bought at a nearby antique store. The truth about what they had really been doing made her ill at ease at first; then, absorbing the new and grown-up atmosphere they were sharing with her in this discussion, she said "Gee!" and then "Really? Oh, wow!"—and seemed not only impressed but rather pleased. As for Ken and Harriet, they resumed their sex life without further difficulty—particularly since Nancy thoughtfully saw to it that she spent many nights at her friend's house for the rest of the summer. The following year, the family rented a bigger and more solid house.

But even if the old tradition is still with us in part, and still capable of doing damage, it has lost much of its former strength.

The change began early in this century, with the decline of prudery, the slow acceptance of the validity of sexual pleasure for its own sake, and the gradual freeing of women from the constraints that blocked their natural sexual responses.

By the 1940's, when Dr. Alfred Kinsey was conducting his monumental survey, he found innumerable indications that people born after the turn of the century tended to have considerably greater freedom in their sexual behavior than those born before 1900. The youngest people in Kinsey's sample showed the most marked change, but even the middle-aged were having a good deal more coitus than the inhibited Victorians had ever had—or than anyone had suspected older people were having in the 1940's. For example, over 97 per cent of the married men in their early 50's, and 94 per cent of those in their late 50's, said they were still having intercourse regularly with their wives. The wives in Kinsey's survey reported somewhat lower incidences—88 and 80 per cent, respectively, for the early and late 50's, with the differences from the male figures being due to differences in sampling and to subjective factors. But even if the truth lay somewhere between the two sets of figures, it was still perfectly clear that the vast majority of middle-aged married people were having intercourse regularly. And reasonably often, too; at age 50 the median (the most typical) rate was still nearly once a week and even in the late 50's was once every couple of weeks.

In fact, there was no sudden end to marital coitus at any age. Speaking of the male, Kinsey reported: "The decline in sexual activity is remarkably steady, and there is no point at which old age suddenly enters the picture." This lifelong decline, Kinsey felt, was due in part to the waning of physiological capacity, but also in part to such mental factors as psychological fatigue and boredom. The female's sexual capability, he said, did not diminish physiologically to the same extent as the male's, nor did her interest, and her marital coital frequency declined chiefly because her husband's activity did.

Kinsey's survey did not show what happened beyond age 60, but a long-term research project of the Duke University Center for the Study of Aging and Human Development did. Once again, the figures proved that by the 1950's the cultural tradition was no longer the impediment it had been earlier. The people in the Duke study ranged in age from 60 to 93 years, and the average age was 70. While the majority of them were sexually inactive, this was because many of them were single, widowed, or divorced. But of those still married and living with their spouses, 54 per cent were sexually active; even beyond age 75, about a quarter of the married contingent still had some continuing sexual activity. As project psychiatrists Gustave Newman and Claude R. Nichols summed up, "Although older people experienced a decline in sexual activity and strength of sexual drive, these data show that, given the conditions of reasonably good health and partners who are also physically active, elderly persons continue to be sexually active into their seventh, eighth, and ninth decades."

Clearly, things had changed, even if few people other than sex researchers realized how much they had. Meanwhile, Dr. William Masters and Mrs. Virginia Johnson, in the Reproductive Biology Research Foundation in St. Louis, were breaking new ground by actually watching, measuring, and recording human sexual behavior in the laboratory. In a series of highly technical papers, and in their 1966 book, *Human Sexual Response,* they provided specific measurements of the physiological changes that take place in middle age and to which we referred earlier in this chapter. But Masters and Johnson reported that the measurable changes in tissues, the slower rate of response to stimuli, and the diminished intensity of orgasmic contractions, were no real bar to sexual activity or enjoyment. And, of course, the changes that often caused mechanical troubles for women can now be taken care of medically. Estrogen replacement by pills or creams restores vaginal tissues and lubrication to their premenopausal condition. Relatively minor surgery, or even simple exercises in some cases, tightens up sagging vaginal muscles—although the use of episiotomies and on-the-spot repairs during birth have made this a diminishing problem. For the rest, nothing about female or male anatomy or physiology (assuming normal health) dictated any end to sexual activity in middle age, or even into the 80's, according to Masters and Johnson.

As far as the older woman was concerned, they were unequivocal:

The aging female is fully capable of sexual performance at orgasmic levels. . . . There seem to be no physiological reasons why the frequency of sexual expression found satisfactory for the younger woman should not be carried over into postmenopausal years.

But if the older married female is dependent for regular coitus upon her husband, doesn't that limit her? Listen to Masters and Johnson speaking of men:

> There is every reason to believe that maintained regularity of sexual expression coupled with adequate physical well-being and healthy mental orientation to the aging process will . . . provide a capacity for sexual performance that frequently may extend to and beyond the 80-year level.

It was only normal, they reported, for a middle-aged man to take longer than a young man to achieve a full erection, to reach orgasm, or to repeat the sex act. But there was no physiological reason for a healthy man to become impotent in middle age, or even later; the problem, if there was one, was usually in his psyche or his habits, not his anatomy. Overwork, fatigue, and, above all, the use of too much alcohol (the greatest single factor associated with secondary impotence in the late 40's or early 50's) were among the most common troublemakers. And then, of course, there is the man's fear (induced by tradition) that he might become impotent in middle age; that fear can make any single episode of poor performance seem to toll the bell. He who thinks he hears the bell toll usually does. But it doesn't have to be.

The Kinsey, Duke, and Masters and Johnson findings have gradually become part of our national heritage of knowledge of sexual behavior, and have done much to free contemporary middle-aged couples from the constraints that tradition used to impose on their sexual behavior. The most recent measurements of the extent to which marital sexuality has cast off the shackles of that tradition can be found in Morton Hunt's book *Sexual Behavior in the 1970s,* a report based on a nationwide questionnaire survey. One of its most striking findings is that the average frequency of coitus by married couples—including the middle-aged—increased considerably between the time of Kinsey's fieldwork (1938–49) and 1972, when the new survey was conducted. Here, in condensed form, are the comparable medians (a median is a midpoint; half of all persons in each age group had less, and half had more, coitus than the median):

MARITAL COITUS: FREQUENCIES PER WEEK, COMBINING MALE AND FEMALE ESTIMATES *

1938–49 (Kinsey)		1972 (Hunt)	
Age	*Median*	*Age*	*Median*
16–25	2.45	18–24	3.25
26–35	1.95	25–34	2.55
36–45	1.40	35–44	2.00
46–55	.85	45–54	1.00
56–60	.50	55 and over	1.00

Note that nowadays, while median frequency still declines among older people, it does so proportionately less than in Kinsey's time. Note, too, that while each age group currently has coitus more often than the same age group in Kinsey's time, *the increase has been proportionately greatest for married people over 55!* And today's 35-to-44 group is more active than the 26-to-35 group of a generation ago.

Certain other hitherto unpublished findings of the 1972 survey indicate that in many ways middle-aged marital sexual behavior is freer now than it was a generation ago. Here are a few typical comparisons between the Kinsey sample and the 1972 sample:

—A generation ago, only a quarter to a third of middle-aged couples had ever used the female-above position during coitus. Today, half to three quarters do so anywhere from occasionally to regularly.

—A generation ago, fewer than one out of ten middle-aged

* Kinsey's data, as given here, are our own adaptation, combining his five-year groupings into ten-year groupings and assuming that the truth lies halfway between the figures based on male estimates and those based on female estimates.

couples had ever used rear-entrance vaginal coitus. Today, between a third and a half do so anywhere from occasionally to regularly.

—A generation ago, fewer than a third of all middle-aged wives had ever performed fellatio on their husbands, and many of these had done so only once or a few times over the years. Today, a third do so, many of them regularly and often.

On all these points, the contemporary young are freer, by far, than the middle-aged, but the latter *do* show up better in one way: according to the 1972 survey, women from their mid-30's to their mid-50's have a higher rate of marital orgasm than their younger counterparts. Evidently, experience counts.

In any case, it is clear that sexual liberation hasn't been only a matter of greater freedom for singles, gays, and far-outs. It has had a major effect upon the overall atmosphere, the practices, and the enjoyment of marital sex—including, and most importantly (from our point of view), that of middle-aged husbands and wives who are now enjoying it almost as much as the hot-blooded young. The 1972 survey asked the respondents how pleasurable they had found marital sex during the past year: 99 per cent of the youngest group of husbands said it had been either very or mostly pleasurable, and the figure dropped only to 94 per cent for the middle-aged groups. Among wives, the highest point was reached by the 35-to-44-year-old group, 93 per cent of whom related it very or mostly pleasurable, and the figure declined insignificantly to 91 per cent for the 45-to-54 group, then moderately to 84 per cent for the 55-and-over group. There are no comparable figures in Kinsey, but judging by everything we've ever heard or read about the enjoyment of married sex in middle age a generation ago, it sounds as if there has been a major gain.

Of course, the survey data and the psychological and medical literature show that there are still a great many middle-aged husbands and wives whose lovemaking is routine, inhibited, boring, and/or spoiled by anxiety, emotional conflicts, or physical problems. We've spoken to many such people—but we've also spoken to a number of middle-aged couples who have a genuinely emancipated and liberated sexual life-style of the kind that we maintain is on the increase. One man and one woman stand out in our memories, and we want you to hear exactly what they said to us, as tape-recorded and faithfully transcribed, with only our questions omitted. First, a genial, beefy electrical-appliance dealer in a Midwestern city, 54 years old, politically a middle-of-the-roader, the father of four, and a now-and-then churchgoer:

I love my sex, and I've got a wife that loves it just as much as me. Our first five years of married life it was every day with us, and sometimes twice a day because my job would allow me to stop off home at lunchtime for a quickie. Nowadays, even after twenty years of marriage, it's still about three times a week—and with the kids finally all in school, we've even started up again on that lunchtime business once in a while. Most of the time, naturally, it's in the evening, after the kids are in bed. My wife puts some of that damned perfume on and I know that she wants it tonight, and that really gets me going. We'll lay on the couch watching TV and playing around with each other and half forgetting about the show. We'll carry on like that, laughing and horsing around, for half an hour or more, and then go to bed and get the bodies together, and it's tremendous. She can wiggle that ass of hers around like you wouldn't believe, and any position I want to use, she couldn't care less. I like doing all kinds of things to her—the only thing I don't do is go down on her, because I had a very bad experience with that when I was in high school and it's had no appeal for me ever since. But all sorts of other things are fine with me. And she does all kinds of things to me, including taking it in her mouth and really working on it. And sometimes I kid her about stuff I've seen in some stag movie the boys have been showing down at the garage, and would you believe she often wants me to *show* her how it went? After all these years?

And now, a 45-year-old blue-collar housewife and mother from a large Eastern city, a Catholic (as is her husband) but, by her own admission, not a strict one:

[After some years of marriage] we felt there was a lot happening that we didn't understand, so I asked my husband if him and I should try to read up on it. So he went out and bought three books, and through them we found all different ways of caressing, and different positions, and it was very nice because we realized that these things weren't dirty. Like I could say to my husband, "Around the world in eighty days!" and he'd laugh and we'd really go at it, relaxed and having fun. And over the years we've continued to find new things—mostly, it's between my husband and I that these new things come about, but also, men talk about sex with each other, you know, and sometimes he'll come home and say, "Here's a thing I just heard about, and let's try it," and I'll say, "Fine," and we do. . . . The position I like best is where I'm on top of my husband and he's caressing me while I'm moving around. That, and also the pillow position, with the pillow under me. And sometimes the both-sitting position. I found that as the children grew older we weren't as free, because they might be awake and listening, but now two are gone, and the third is out late sometimes, so we have more chances to be a little wild at times. . . . What gets me wild? Sometimes I'll read a book, and there's a sex scene in it, and the stimulation is there and I can't wait for my husband to come home, I mean I'd be lying if I said otherwise. And me 45—now isn't that something? I'll bet my Mom and Dad didn't carry on like that when they were my age. I *know* they didn't, because once she said they all but stopped for good when she began getting her change.

Let's be honest; not everyone has learned to make as much of middle-aged sexuality as these people. But if everyone had, there wouldn't be much point in our writing this chapter; so for those who would welcome them, we would like to offer a few specific suggestions.

Obviously, if any medical problems exist—painful intercourse, abnormal discharge, itching, burning, postcoital soreness in the female; painful ejaculation, urethritis, or postcoital prostatic discomfort in the male—it is of the utmost importance to consult a qualified physician. But not one who tells you that it's natural to become a sexual dropout at your age. In Chapter 7 we'll have more to say about health, and about the medical treatment of some common conditions, but right now we would like to lay to rest some of the fears many middle-aged people have about the relationship of certain illnesses to sexual capacity.

—Hysterectomy does not spell the end of sexual desire, capacity, or the ability to receive pleasure through any means that were enjoyed before. Even if the ovaries have been removed, with estrogen-replacement therapy the tissues of the vagina and vulva should be as healthy as ever, and although there is no longer a womb to contract at orgasm, the orgasm can still be just as deeply satisfying, physically and psychologically, as it was before surgery.

—Prostatectomy only rarely affects erectile ability and has little or no physiological effect upon libido or sexual arousability. Although the quantity of ejaculate is lessened, in most cases overall sexual performance is otherwise unchanged, with orgasm still capable of yielding complete satisfaction.

—Diabetic men have a higher incidence of impotence, and diabetic women of frigidity, than nondiabetics; this is a matter of concern to those in mid-life because it is at this time that adult diabetes most commonly makes its appearance. Even in the absence of other symptoms, a sudden loss of sexual interest might be good reason to ask your doctor to check your glucose tolerance. If you do have diabetes-caused sexual difficulties, as soon as the diabetes is brought under proper control by diet or drugs, those difficulties should disappear.

—Heart ailments in both males and females may be an impediment to sexual activity because of the patient's fear of worsening his condition. Such anxiety is usually unnecessary, for few doctors now prohibit intercourse even for persons who have had severe heart attacks except during the initial period of convalescence. For one thing, research has shown that the stress of unrelieved sexual tension does more harm than the activity itself. For another, according to Drs. Ernest Friedman and Herman Hellerstein of Case Western Reserve University, the pulse rate does not rise more than it does during many other routine activities, and the period of maximum acceleration usually lasts only about 15 seconds; they conclude that "Over 80 per cent of men [and, presumably, women] who have had coronaries can fulfill the demands of sexual activity without evidence of significant strain."

There are, of course, many other varieties of heart disorder, but few of them need interfere with coitus if care is exercised to choose sexual techniques which will reduce the amount of physical effort involved; for all cardiac patients, it is not the orgasm per se that causes fatigue and strain on the heart, but rather the prolonged and energetic effort that precedes it. Any pair of sexual partners can easily modify their behavior so that physical effort is minimized without impairing pleasure or satisfaction. One way is to have an extended period of foreplay and only a brief period of intromission and energetic movement. Another is to interrupt the period of coital movement for many brief periods of rest; even a few seconds at a time is helpful. Each couple has to evolve its own modifications, but any couple that wants to can do so. And love it.

In the absence of any real medical problems, the answer to successful middle-aged sex is twofold: first, *enlightenment*—the casting out of unfounded fears and erroneous beliefs; and second, *adaptation*—minor modifications of technique to accommodate to the physiological changes that time does bring. We have already had enough to say about enlightenment, but there are a few practical suggestions that can be made about adaptation:

First, any postmenopausal woman who has inadequate lubrication can use a small dab of surgical lubricating jelly. Even better, plain saliva is probably the closest thing to the vagina's own secretions and it is natural, handy—and free. Besides, having it applied directly by oral-genital contact is exciting and delightful to both partners, assuming that it is a technique acceptable to both of them. For medical correction of slow or inadequate vaginal lubrication, estrogen tablets or topical creams eliminate the problem altogether, but these products can be obtained only by prescription and should be used under the supervision of a gynecologist or family physician.

Second, since both middle-aged men and women are slower to respond and to be ready for intercourse, longer and more inventive foreplay is in order. Unfortunately, many people are unaware of this simple truth; when they fail to become aroused with the lightning speed of youth, they become uneasy, or fully alarmed, and this only works against them. As Dr. Masters points out, the older man is slower to run around the block than he was in his 20's and does not worry about it, "yet the fact that it takes him a little longer to have an erection scares him to death"—and his anxiety is his undoing.

What does one do during a longer period of foreplay? We needn't review here all the many ways of looking, touching, caressing, nibbling, nuzzling, kissing, tasting, inhaling, massaging; there is a glut of books on the market that will supplement your own repertoire with more ideas than you will ever need. Among them, however, we recommend as two high-quality sources the sober, professional discussion of techniques of "sensate focus" to be found throughout the second Masters-Johnson book, *Human Sexual Inadequacy*, and the very readable, often poetic descriptions of sexual techniques in *The Joy of Sex* edited by Dr. Alex Comfort. The best thing about many of these variations is that they aren't just means to an end; they are ends in themselves—activities so pleasing that the middle-aged couple may well wish to linger for lingering's sake. And after all, that is the very essence of the art of love as advocated and taught for many centuries in other societies more sensuous than our own.

Third, the middle-aged must pay particular attention to their overall physical condition. Alcohol, as the bawdy porter in *Macbeth* pointed out, "provokes the desire, but it takes away the performance"—especially in men, and more especially in middle-aged men. Masters and Johnson assert that many a case of middle-aged impotence is begun by a single episode of erectile feebleness due to alcohol, which is then magnified and perpetuated by fear and anxiety. So it's a good idea to go easy on drink when planning to have sex. It might also be a good idea to go to bed early, since fatigue, too, can interfere severely with sexual response in either sex. If the latter suggestion happens to be impractical at times, the alternatives are to make love before dinner (why not, if there aren't any children around?), in the morning, or after an hour's sleep.

Fourth, it is normal for the middle-aged man to have a less intense need for orgasm than the young man. This means that he is definitely slower in arriving at the culmination of the coital act —and all of the experts, and most of our interviewees, consider this a real boon. As one man put it, "I can remember the 'good old days' when I was forever desperately whispering, 'Hold it! Don't move! —oh, *goddamn!*—oh, I'm *sorry*, dear!' What an improvement now. I can go on as long as I like, and never lose control." Which is splendid—except that some men get apprehensive and panicky when, on occasion, they have a little difficulty finally reaching orgasm. But a deft caress by the wife, in just the right place, often triggers off the reluctant orgasm at once. Each person has his own "right" place, and if his wife doesn't know where it is, it's time to let her in on the secret. For some men it's the testes, for others, the perineum, and for still others, the buttocks and especially the region right around the anus. The most important thing of all is to bear in mind that doctors now say there is absolutely no cause for alarm if orgasm is sometimes difficult for the middle-aged man to achieve, or if, occasionally, he fails to have one at all. It is physiologically normal, does not signify any disorder, and definitely will not cause physical harm or discomfort as it might in a young man.

Finally, according to Masters and Johnson, the most effective way of preserving sexual capacity is *regular and frequent sexual activity* itself. People who don't eat for long periods of time get shrunken stomachs and a decreased ability to accept and digest food; athletes who stop participating in athletics lose their muscle tone, stamina, and skill. And people who fail to engage in any form of sexual activity over a long period of time lose their sexual appetites, their skills, and the responsiveness of the muscles and tissues that are used in sexual activity. All of those appetites, skills, and physical responses can be regained, as Masters and Johnson's clinical accounts show, but it takes time, effort, and, often, costly professional guidance to do so; it's a far better idea not to let your sexual machinery deteriorate in the first place.

Masters and Johnson found that older women who had not been engaging regularly in either intercourse or masturbation frequently did encounter problems when they attempted coitus; but by contrast, older women—even those over 60—who had remained sexually active generally had no difficulties even when, upon inspection, their vaginal tissues appeared to show signs of estrogen deprivation. Similarly, older males who had remained sexually active tended to preserve their physiological responses, while those who had become inactive did not. In Dr. David Reuben's catchphrase, "Use it or lose it." The only thing wrong with the slogan is its failure to mention that even when lost, "it" can usually be regained.

"It does not appear to matter what manner of sexual expression has been employed," Masters and Johnson add, "as long as high levels of activity were maintained." What that means should be obvious: even when, for one reason or another, coitus is temporarily inappropriate or impossible—as, for example, when one member of the couple is ill—it is better not to let a long period go by without some form of sexual activity. The incapacitated partner, if not too ill, can stimulate the other manually or orally to the point of orgasm, and take pleasure and pride in doing so. Or either partner can, in all good conscience, masturbate privately from time to time until coitus can be resumed. Masturbation under such circumstances is not only a way to relieve individual sexual tension (which would be justification enough) but something more important: a way of preserving physiological abilities and therefore of ensuring the successful resumption of a full sexual relationship as soon as possible. Obviously, too, this is particularly applicable to those without regular partners—the single, divorced, and widowed.

Our advocacy of masturbation may strike some of our readers as absurd, and a few as mildly shocking. But for those who haven't heard the news, the attitude of sex experts and psychologists toward this practice has changed a great deal in recent years. They no longer regard it merely as an acceptable *substitute* for coitus in adolescence, but rather as an acceptable *supplement* to coitus in adult life when needed, provided it is not used compulsively or as a bar to marital relations. The general public, especially the younger generation of adults, has become quite tolerant of masturbation, but a fair number of middle-aged people still consider it vaguely shameful or even abnormal in people their own age, particularly those who are married. Many others, however, though they hide the fact, agree with the young and masturbate when they need to or merely want to. According to hitherto unpublished data from the 1972 survey, in the 45-to-54 age range, 35 per cent of husbands and 24 per cent of wives masturbated in the past year, most of them at least a few times. Above the age of 55, the percentages are somewhat smaller—26 per cent for husbands, 14 per cent for wives—but even these figures are much higher than those of a generation ago. (Far larger percentages of younger married people masturbate, but that is to be expected; they're more sexually liberated in most ways than middle-aged people.)

But there's much more to sex in middle age than a mere preservation of capabilities or a continuation of what went before; if it weren't so, we wouldn't have called this chapter "Passionate Middle Age." We firmly believe that for many people, middle age can bring a significant resurgence or increase of sexual pleasure and a revitalization and intensification of the sexual relationship, concomitant with the deepening and refinement of the personal relationship. We believe that middle age can be, and *ought* to be, a passionate time of life. And for good reasons.

Not in many years have the postparental husband and wife had so much time to enjoy each other as companions, to rediscover the pleasures of doing things together, become newly intimate, feel and demonstrate affection.

Not in many years have they had so much privacy to engage in little (and major) verbal and physical intimacies, spontaneously and freely.

Never before—not even when they were young and childless— have they had the leisure and the motivation they now have to concentrate on learning about their own and each other's bodily reactions and emotional responses, to cultivate the giving and receiving of delight, and to add to their repertoire many sexual acts they may have been too inhibited, or too set in their ways, to try before.

Never before has the wife (unless she has had a hysterectomy) been wholly free of the fear of pregnancy and the inconvenience of the menses; never before has the husband had better control over his own responses or been as able to prolong coitus for his own pleasure and his wife's.

Never before have both partners had as good reason to be leisurely, sensuous, and sensual, nor has the slowness of either one been less of an imposition on the other.

Never before have the sexual responses of the man and the woman been so closely attuned to each other. As psychiatrists

Helen Kaplan and Clifford Sager point out, "Older males become more like women in their sexual behavior in that fantasy and ambience become more important in lovemaking, and there is less preoccupation with orgasm.... Psychic determinants become heavier contributors to the final sexual response." If the sexuality of middle age isn't as wild and desperate as the sexuality of youth, it has, instead, its own special quality of tender, meaningful, and harmonious passion.

For all these reasons, we believe that middle age can be a Prime Time for sex—not in terms of maximum performance, or impressive scores, but in terms of sharing and caring, of becoming part of each other's bodies and minds, of loving and delighting, of understanding and being understood. In a word—an often misused word—a Prime Time for *making love.*

But although it is just that for a growing number of middle-aged persons, it isn't for all too many others. Not only are fears and misconceptions about middle-aged sexual capacity still common, but by mid-life, after years devoted to child-rearing and the career struggle, many people have become relative strangers to each other. This loss in companionate intimacy is closely allied to a loss of erotic intimacy: the decline of either one causes the decline of the other, but conversely, the preservation or rediscovery of either one reawakens or enhances the other.

Bernice comments

There was a time, not long ago, when some sociologists—and a good many other people—believed that marriages high in companionship were low in sex. Partners in such alliances might be good pals, but surely their erotic interests would flourish only where there were maximum male-female differences, as in a Tarzan-Jane relationship.

With the recent growth of sex equality and the easing of rigid sex roles, it has become much more commonly accepted that the most companionable marriages are also the most sexually vital.

I, for one, did not need to be convinced on this point—but my preexisting conviction was strongly reinforced during the last few years. In the course of touring the country to interview hundreds of women for Morton's sex survey, and later for this book, I was more and more struck, as I listened to the women speak, by the evidence of the intertwining of overall intimacy and sexuality in marriage.

When we set out on the first tour, I had had no previous experience as an interviewer. Morton, who had had a great deal, carefully trained me for the work, but in spite of his reassurances I couldn't really believe that women would be willing to talk to a total stranger about intimate sexual matters; I even had anxious fantasies about long, miserable silences in which the only sound to be heard would be the motor of the tape recorder. Happily, it worked out very differently from my gloomy prediction.

Although the interviewees were all anonymous, they *were* facing a stranger and a microphone, and most of them appeared to be tense and anxious at first. But using my new training, I would first chat about general topics, offer some information about the project, and give the woman time to relax and become acquainted. When my questions began, the first ones were simple and neutral (When and where were you born? What did your mother and father do?). From then on, the questioning advanced, by gentle stages, through childhood and adolescence and into the present; at no point was there any sudden leap into difficult territory, but usually, in less than an hour, we would be talking about almost incredibly intimate details of the interviewee's sexual activities with her husband—or nonmarital partner or partners—and her feelings about them.

By the end of the two-hour session the tape recorder had long been forgotten, and the talk flowed easily as between old friends; often, there was the distinct impression that a real and warm relationship had been established. Even now, after several years, I remember most of those women vividly, and with sympathy and, often, affection. I believe that genuine feelings between us developed so quickly because we were dealing with deeply personal information in an absolutely anonymous, "safe" way, with no pretense of any kind and nothing held back. We were truly intimate in a limited and special fashion.

But in spite of the similarities in overall ambience at each interview, these women were very different from each other in their internal reactions to the situation. When the two hours were over and I had to conclude the meeting, some women simply stood up, shook hands, said goodbye, and left. But others were most reluctant to go.

They said such things as, "You're a total stranger and yet I've told you things I've never told anyone in my whole life before." Many wanted to know if we could meet again. (We could not.) Some wept and said they felt emotional but marvelous, too, and wonderfully enriched by having been able to talk about it all; they thanked me (while *I* was trying to thank *them*) and said that I had helped them a great deal. But I hadn't done anything except ask just enough questions to get them started and listen sympathetically while they talked. I offered no advice (except in a few cases when I suggested that they see a therapist), and only occasionally passed along some basic information from field studies.

Why, then, did some of these interviewees become so deeply involved with me? I had only to listen to the first few tapes to understand the pattern: the ones who had the most powerful reactions, the deepest feelings of interaction, the greatest sense of benefit from talking freely and openly about their own sexuality, were the ones who lacked an intimate relationship with their husbands or lovers. They had never talked to them as they had talked to me—and these women were the very ones whose sex lives were dull, or non-existent, or thoroughly unsatisfactory in some other way. The others, who spoke freely but without urgency, without grasping at instant intimacy, without tears, were the ones who, by and large, had warm, intimate relationships with the men in their lives—and almost always healthy, good, and often great sexual relationships.

Morton comments

I can second Bernice's observations, but with a difference. I've been interviewing both men and women about their sexual attitudes and experiences for nearly a dozen years, and I have found that very few men are as freely able as most women to admit—even to themselves—how closely intimacy is allied to their own sexual passion. But I've definitely come away with the very strong impression that for most middle-aged men, good marital sex is strongly dependent upon a close, trusting, and deeply companionable relationship. A number of young men have told me about the marvelous or prodigious bouts of sex they were having with their wives, even though the emotional relationship was poor, but I've almost never heard a middle-aged man say that marital sex was good where the emotional relationship was not. Why this difference? One reason might be the sheer machismo of the young male: it's vital to him to make it in a big way, no matter what. Another might be that the Oedipal conflict in young boys splits love and sex far apart, and it takes many years of adult life to bring them back together. Still another might be that as the sexual responsiveness of the male begins to diminish in middle age, he tends to function best where he feels emotionally secure; accordingly, he loses "interest" or even potency in a poor relationship, but retains it—and becomes aware of the importance of the connection—in a good one.

How can the middle-aged couple make the most of the passionate potential of their middle years? We have offered a number of suggestions already and named two of the most useful books we know on the subject. But we have one more thought on the matter: for those whose sex life is stuck in a rut or lacking in excitement or intensity, it may be necessary to do more than borrow a few ideas —it may be better to make a deliberate, consciously programed fresh start.

The key to making such a new beginning is to become newly *aware* of each other as persons and as sexual partners. In many sensitivity-training groups, encounter groups, and marital-counseling and sex-therapy clinics, husbands and wives with stale relationships and stale sex lives are taught how to stop and take a new look at each other (and themselves), how to perceive each other again as if meeting for the first time, and how to start building a new sexual and emotional intimacy. Borrowing from such sources —the more important of which are named in the bibliography—we offer a few suggestions for making such a start on your own; each of these suggestions has been tested by various kinds of therapists and found useful. (If, however, your problem is a severe one—consisting of frequent or chronic frigidity, impotence, premature ejaculation, painful intercourse, and the like—you will almost certainly require professional assistance, a subject dealt with in Chapter 7.)

Step One in rediscovering each other, and in rekindling sexual excitement within marriage, is the hardest: You have to agree, jointly, that things aren't what they could be, and that you want to make the effort to rebuild. That calls for open and honest talk—and if open and honest communication hasn't been your habit, it won't be easy. We don't know any way to make it easy. You might, of course, just leave this book, open to this page, on the coffee table and hope—but since you can't make any progress at all without real communication, you might as well take the plunge and start to talk right from the beginning.

Step Two: Each one has to make a genuine effort to be attractive, interesting, charming—just as a single person does when meeting a new potential partner. This means taking a good look at your clothes, skin, hair, body posture—and doing something about whatever could use improvement. Some new clothes, a new hairstyle, a program of regular exercise, will make you feel more interesting and exciting to yourself—and it's bound to project outward. Then something much more difficult: instead of the routine chit-chat that can easily fill an evening, make an effort to talk to each other about things that *matter*—bygone but important experiences; current experiences that are charged with emotional or intellectual values; worries, fears, and hopes; Big Issues. In short, the kind of talk you would make with a dear friend you hadn't seen in a long while—or with a new friend you really want to become close to.

Step Three (which is concurrent with Two): The two of you agree that you are seeking to rekindle and revivify your sex life—but that temporarily you will postpone actual intercourse until *both* of you want it very much; first you are going to employ a number of techniques of increasing your awareness and sensitivity, and of creating sexual excitement. You pledge to each other that until you have done these things, you will hold off on actual coitus. How long? In many sex-therapy clinics, it may be for a number of days, or a week, or even more. For you, since you don't have a problem of acute sexual failure, it might be an hour, a day, a couple of days— whatever you both agree on and need. (If you will recall how it was when, for some reason, you *couldn't* have sex—when one of you was sick, or shortly before and after the birth of a child—you'll remember how desperately you wanted to, just because you couldn't. So agreeing on a moratorium while you carry out preliminary procedures will be valuable in itself; moreover, it will make it easier to do arousing things if you know that, temporarily, neither of you has to carry through and achieve some resounding success.)

Step Four: Start doing things that will enhance your mood. Go out to dinner festively; hold hands at the table (if you feel like it); kiss or embrace, talk about sex and about other things that excite you. When you get home and feel the urge, try some general sensitivity play—pregenital forms of arousal; not just whatever you've always done, but things you've rarely or never done, borrowing ideas from *Human Sexual Inadequacy, The Joy of Sex,* and other good books of technique. You might, for instance, try washing each other, massaging each other's bodies with fragrant oils, looking at yourselves in a mirror as you stroke each other—all the while telling each other what feels good, how good it feels, what things you like best, what things you would like to try.

Step Five: When these activities lead to sexual excitement in both of you, move on to actual genital activity—not coitus, but various kinds of caresses with fingers, lips,. tongue; again, they're described in detail in the sources we've named. Ask each other, and tell each other, what works. Even if you have been married for many years, it is quite possible that neither of you really knows the optimum way of exciting the other sexually, but only the fairly good way that you settled on long ago. No one but the owner of a clitoris really knows what way of touching it feels best to her, or whether she doesn't like it touched at all but prefers the stroking of the surrounding area; no one but the owner of a penis can say exactly what speed, pressure, or localized attention does the most to please and excite him. So tell each other. If you need to, and can, *show* each other. Why not? It's an intimate, endearing, and exciting thing to do if each of you trusts the other enough to overcome your initial embarrassment. Take turns just making each other feel good. Spend five or ten or any number of minutes with one person doing everything possible to give pleasure to the other and the recipient doing nothing but enjoying it all, and expressing that enjoyment. At the end of the allotted time, turn about; giver and receiver trade roles.

Step Six: Perhaps that same night, or perhaps not until the next night, or even later, but only when you *both* feel so impatient that you can't wait any longer—it's time for intercourse. But first agree, and say it out loud, that the important thing is just to enjoy doing it;

there is no other goal. Nobody has to have an orgasm, let alone the greatest orgasm in history, and certainly not more than one. Nobody has to keep intercourse going for five minutes, ten minutes, an hour and a quarter. Nobody has to use six different positions, or any set number of them. Nobody has to go mad with ecstasy. Any such goals are apt to be self-defeating because they engender anxiety about performance and achievement. This is neither a performance nor a test. Just enjoy your own sensations and each other's, and all the things you've learned about each other's bodies and feelings. And if, after a while, either partner begins to feel swept away toward culmination, don't try to hold back or slow down; just let it happen. If the other partner is swept along by it, that's great; if not, you can start again later, or the partner who didn't get there can be lovingly assisted by the one who did. The main thing is that a grand and satisfying experience for one partner is that for both (as long as it isn't always the same one). The next time, it may be the other partner who has the coital orgasm or, happily, both. But any way of having sex that both partners enjoy, any way that yields each one the pleasure both of getting and of giving to the other, any way that ends in mutual release, is good. And in a truly loving relationship, it is the beginning of building a passionate middle age.

We cannot conclude this discussion without saying a few words about another and wholly different way of pursuing the goal of passionate middle age. This is the search for more intense, varied, and revitalizing experience by means of sexual relations outside of the marriage.

In recent years, not only has the public become somewhat more tolerant of extramarital activity, but extramarital relationships have been touted as a benefit to the individual, and even as the very salvation of marriage, by people ranging from serious social scientists to flamboyant sexual anarchists, and from militant feminists to believers in the Playboy Philosophy. Many of the advocates of extramarital relations are concerned primarily with the justification of secret sexual affairs; others, more interestingly, argue that in order to bring marriage into line with present-day realities and social conditions, extramarital relations should be recognized and licit, whether in the form of individual outside relationships ("permissive marriage," or "open marriage"), switching and co-marital sex, or swinging and group sex.

The arguments for extramarital freedom, especially of the open and licit variety, make one or more of these points:

—The concept of sexual fidelity is essentially that of a *property right*, in which each partner obtains an exclusive franchise over the other's sexual services. This is an obsolete notion, and totally out of harmony with contemporary attitudes toward the self and toward interpersonal relationships. Neither partner can rightfully *possess* the other; each always retains the right to use his or her body as he or she sees fit.

—The notion that sex is indissolubly tied in with love and marriage is a mere cultural prejudice. Sex can be part of love and marriage—but it can also be enjoyed apart from either one, like any other appetite. And enjoying it thus not only adds to one's total pleasure, but keeps marriage from becoming a confinement and a form of self-denial.

—The human being, like other animals, is sexually stimulated and revitalized by change and variety. After some years of marriage, the accustomed partner has a diminished ability to arouse, while a new partner (or series of partners) can reawaken sexual desire, capacity, and awareness. Besides, sexual renewal makes the individual feel renewed in other ways—young, desirable, successful.

—For marriage to survive today, it must be reconstructed to fit modern conditions. To avoid isolation, confinement, and stagnation, we need to go outside marriage for enrichment, broader experience, growth. And when this is done by mutual consent, it only makes the spouses closer to each other, because they share their experiences with each other.

Well, those are the major arguments, and we could spend a whole chapter considering them. But this isn't the place for that; our interest here is in assessing the usefulness of this approach for the middle-aged. In doing so, we are not at all concerned with how the extramarital alternatives hold up in the light of religious or other formal codes of ethics; our concern is pragmatic—we judge this approach solely in terms of the likelihood that it will enrich and intensify the sexual life of the middle-aged person without undue cost or without damaging other aspects of life that count for as much or more. With that limitation in mind, we'd like to comment on the four major arguments, one by one.

—First, we agree completely that in the context of modern life, marriage should not imply possession by either partner of the other or the acquisition of property rights over the other's sexual being. Sexual exclusivity in marriage should be voluntary and a matter of mutual agreement. If partner A insists on exclusivity against partner B's strong wishes, the marriage will seem coercive to B; but if partner B has extramarital affairs against A's strong wishes, then the marriage will seem flawed and unsound to A. However, if A and B agree that each is free to have outside relationships, there need be no bar to them—if they do not turn out to make trouble for either partner. As far as we can see, this is as true for the middle-aged as for the young—except, we think, that it is much more apt to make trouble in middle age. We'll comment on that a little later.

—Second, the argument that sex can be detached from love and marriage is simply not backed up by the biological, psychological, and anthropological evidence. In infancy, we first learn to associate creature comfort and sensuous good feeling with love, and the connection is ineradicably imprinted on us. As adults, we may be capable at times of having sex experiences—even, indeed, powerful ones—without any emotional attachment to the partner, but this is the exception, not the rule. The normal tendency—and it has been true in most human societies, not just our own—is for intense sexual experiences to generate emotional ties, and for powerful emotional feelings to arouse sexual desire. That's why the history of extramarital behavior is filled with stories of a mere romp turning into a great love affair that damages or destroys the marriage. Incidentally, according to sociologist John Cuber and others, the closer the marriage, the more likely an extramarital relationship is to ruin it.

All this applies with particular force to the marriages of the middle-aged. What is emotionally threatening to the young is all the more so to the middle-aged, for whom the thought of marital breakdown is far more alarming. There seems so much more to lose (in terms of years invested), so much less chance of finding another partner and rebuilding one's life. And the extramarital involvements of the middle-aged are more apt to have special impact, for often the discontented wanderer is not just seeking a passing thrill, but desperately trying to grasp at what seems like one last chance at making the most of life. Accordingly, the middle-aged person's affair is often invested with more importance—and more potential danger to the marriage—than the younger person's affair.

Even when sex outside of marriage is supposedly disjoined from emotion, and mutually permitted (as in swinging and group sex), the assumption that each spouse will be as free and as well rewarded by that freedom as the other almost never proves to be true. Very rarely are both partners equally capable of attracting others, equally sure of their own appeal, equally successful in obtaining sexual satisfaction from relations with mere acquaintances or strangers. And almost always, the partner who is less rewarded will be discontented, jealous—and anxious, wondering whether the other is finding strangers who are more appealing, more exciting, more desirable. All of this applies with special force to the middle-aged woman, who is particularly apt to feel threatened by younger, firmer, prettier women; and to the middle-aged man, who is particularly apt to feel threatened by younger, leaner, more virile men.

—The third argument—that change and variety stimulate and revitalize sexual capacity—is undoubtedly true for some people. Probably every one of us has known some middle-aged and sexually bored husband who, falling into an affair, finds himself to be a superstud and experiences long-forgotten, or perhaps previously unknown, transports; and probably every one of us has known some middle-aged wife who, in the arms of a new man, finds herself so overwhelmed by ecstasy that she is all but unappeasable.

The trouble with this remedy for the jaded appetite is that it is like an addictive drug: it requires continual doses. If novelty is the stimulus, one can never reach the goal of the passionate life, but must always be pursuing it in the form of another new partner, and then another, and yet another. To find the time, the psychic and physical energy, the money, and the opportunity is hard enough for the young single person, but is almost impossible, and an overwhelming burden, for the middle-aged married person. Worse still, the hazards of this pursuit are particularly severe in middle age—the risk of rejection in favor of a younger competitor, the risk of ridicule or social disgrace, the risk of psychic damage arising from sexual incompatibility with the stranger. This last is particularly important: given the special sexual needs of the middle-aged that we have discussed, it should be clear that many, if not most, middle-aged people do best with sexual partners whose needs complement their own, who understand their feelings and capabilities, whose acceptance and love enable them to function effectively and joyously. That's rarely the case with a stranger, a new partner, or one who is much younger.

Morton comments

Among the men and women I have interviewed about their extramarital experiences, a fair number have spoken of them as yielding extraordinary sexual pleasure. But a good many others have told me that in such encounters novelty and variety produce anxiety, inhibition, and insecurity, with the result that the men often have potency problems, and the women often fail to feel sexual arousal or to reach orgasm. The mental and emotional excitement of extramarital activity may be intense, but the physical performance of both the men and the women is often distinctly inferior to that which they manifest with their spouses. I have the very strong impression that such negative effects are far more common in middle-aged people than in younger ones.

Even for those whose extramarital encounters are successful, each experience is only a temporary expedient. The risks and the difficulties grow greater with the passing years and eventually become worrisome even to the most enthusiastic advocate of extramarital activity. I've met only a handful of men and women who have sought variety extramaritally for years without losing their taste for it. I've met many who continued to do so for years because they had a compulsion to do so—but they themselves would admit that it was hardly a joyous and passionate way of sexual life.

—The fourth argument, that contemporary marriage tends to be isolating unless each partner can enrich his life by outside experience, is sound and we agree heartily with it. Indeed, it is a major theme in this book that in middle age, more than ever before, men and women should expand their interests, try things they have never tried before, involve themselves in new and important outside relationships.

But we don't agree that this should extend to love relationships or sexual relationships. Same-sex friendships, business friendships, and alliances with others in community and political affairs are distinctly different in their nature, and in their meaning for the marriage, from romantic or sexual involvements. The former do not compete with the essential husband-wife bond; in fact, they generally add to it by enriching the husband-wife exchange of experience and ideas. But romantic and/or sexual involvements are something else; they do compete with and threaten the marital alliance, and draw off some part of the emotional identification within the marriage and invest it elsewhere.

And this, we feel, is particularly true of the middle-aged. It is in mid-life that the sexual and emotional ties between spouses need especially loving attention, for with the departure of the children, many of the old ties that held the partners together are loosened. It may be that the marriage has become so hollow, by this point, that it is not worth saving or protecting; in that case, extramarital involvement can hardly be criticized. If, however, the marriage is fundamentally valuable but merely faded, extramarital relationships are definitely not the way to restore its luster. Middle age is a time for enriching, not impoverishing, the relationship; for the ripening and perfecting of the central bond in one's life, not the endless pursuit of new and transient ties; for the deepening of trust and compassion, not the accentuation of suspicion and self-centeredness; for the maximizing of each partner's trust in the other, not the maximizing of grounds for doubt.

Above all, it is a time for the cultivation of the values of maturity—wisdom, understanding, empathy, self-respect; and the rekindling of sexual passion should take place in ways that are compatible with these values.

And yet we agree, and do not think it contradicts our general thesis, that under certain conditions there are definite benefits to be derived from extramarital activity. It can be a form of testing to see whether one's sexual capacity, defective in marriage, is so because of a flawed marriage relationship but is normal outside it. It can provide change, reassurance, and relief when a marriage is stalemated or hard to endure but cannot, for some reason, be dissolved. It can be a transitional step from a defunct or decaying marriage to the single state and, eventually, to a more successful marriage. It can bring about a physical reawakening and a new awareness of a sexual potential that has not been achieved within the marriage —and this new awareness may ultimately redound to the benefit of the marriage.

But these are all temporary uses of extramarital activity; it does not seem to us to be a viable *way of life*—at least not for the great majority of the middle-aged. Some may be able to make it work, in one form or another, for a while, but very few will be able to make it work indefinitely, or without great cost. It is our considered opinion that passionate middle age can almost always best be achieved in conjunction with the rediscovery of companionate intimacy and the rebuilding of the one-to-one couple relationship.

5 *The Experience Elite*

THE PSYCHOLOGICAL AND
SOCIAL ADVANTAGES OF HAVING
LIVED AND LEARNED

What incomparable asset does every middle-aged person have that no younger one has?

A minimum of forty years of life experience.

There's no substitute for it, no way to acquire it short of living and learning. You've heard of the social elite and the power elite, but you probably never realized that as a middle-aged person you, too, are a member of a special and privileged group—the experience elite.

Your four or more decades of experience, unlike mileage on a car, aren't just wear and tear; though some experiences damage or deplete us, by far the largest part of them add to—and improve—the basic mechanism. They constitute a massive accumulation of emotional, social, and intellectual equipment—a unique asset, quite different from, and in many ways more valuable than, talent, ambition, or energy. For even the talented, the ambitious, and the energetic, if they lack experience, are capable of making innumerable minor or even major misjudgments and mistakes—and they know it; it's what makes life so difficult for the young, no matter what their other advantages. Nothing is a substitute for the judgment, the wisdom, the inner certainty, the ease and swiftness of decision-making in all sorts of situations, that come from decades of interplay between the human organism and the outside world. "Experience is the best teacher" is a well-worn cliché, but it is overfamiliar precisely because it is a profound truth that has been rediscovered and resaid countless times by countless people.

We human animals are equipped with fewer built-in instinctual behavior patterns and automatic responses than any other species; this is why experience is so important to us. Through experience, rather than through innate reactions, we come to behave in ways that ensure our survival and maximize our satisfactions. The process begins at birth: by means of our many random responses to pain and pleasure, sights and sounds, internal and external sensations, and our recognition that some of those responses bring better results than others, we learn how to get attention and food, to grasp objects, to crawl, stand, walk, and talk, to win approval and avoid disapproval, to communicate in speech, and to exert some degree of control over other people. Through experience, not instinct, we come to know that fire is hot, that falling down the steps hurts, that hitting a playmate may result in our being hit in return, that some kinds of behavior bring punishment and other kinds rewards.

And that's only the beginning. Through speech and reading, at play and in school, in our friendships and enmities, we go on to learn ever more complicated things throughout childhood and adulthood. The content and method of our learning changes as time passes, but the fundamental process never ends; formal education is completed, for most people, by early adulthood, but informal education continues until the final declining years.

The part of our informal education that takes place during the young adult years, away from the parental home, has a special importance. It is not until we have completed our formal schooling and our social apprenticeship that we finally begin to perform, in real life, the roles we have been studying. We slowly become more skilled and at ease in them as we discover how other people react to us and as we begin to enlarge and refine our repertoire of social and career behavior. We gradually manage to integrate all that we had previously learned with what we are learning now.

By middle age, in addition to the schoolroom and social learning of the first two decades of life, we have completed two more decades of reality-based social and technical experience as young single adults, as lovers, as husbands and wives, as parents, as workers, as friends, as members of the community, as mourners of the dead. By middle age we are, for the first time in our lives, essentially completed human beings, experienced in nearly all the major aspects of life. And this is why, contrary to the cultural mythology of middle age, psychological and sociological surveys show that most middle-aged people feel more self-assured, confident, in charge of themselves, and capable of dealing with their immediate environment than do young people.

During the transition to middle age, to be sure, many of us go through a period—grossly mislabeled "the middle-aged crisis" by some writers—of difficult reappraisal, uncertainty, even disorientation, but after that transition period the typical middle-aged person is likely to have a sense of certainty about himself and the world, to feel that he knows how to deal with most situations, to be reasonably certain what results his behavior will foster. For after all, he has known so many other human beings, had so many varied experiences, tested so many possible ways of behaving, that he is almost always in a comparatively familiar and understandable situation. In middle age one rarely flounders about or vacillates, uncertain of the right course or the probable consequences of one's choices; one knows at last who one is, feels a sense of security in performing one's part. In Paul Tillich's classic phrase, one has "the courage to be."

And that courage, deriving from our experience, is reflected by the world around us, from which we receive a new kind of response in middle age: the respect, deference, and esteem accorded us as members of the experience elite, as students fully graduated from the university of life. What people around us recognize is that the accumulation of experience has produced in us a high level of *judgment*. The great Samuel Johnson once remarked, in fact, "As a man advances in life he gets what is better than admiration—judgment to estimate things at their own value"—but actually one gets both judgment *and* admiration: not the visceral response to a glowing complexion or a beautiful physique, but the emotional and intellectual appreciation of one's human ripeness and completeness.

Yet is it really true that we middle-aged are highly valued in our society and have psychological, social, and professional advantages over the young? Doesn't that run counter to what we read and hear every day about America's being a "youth culture"? And did we not say earlier in this book that American society was youth-oriented from the beginning and has been so ever since?

What we said about America's beginnings was correct: there were relatively few older people in the nation in its early years, and during the twin social explosions of technology and immigration the young were better able to adapt and to fit into the evolving American society than many of their elders. But this was true only of certain areas of social life; elsewhere—indeed, in most of the fundamental values and norms of behavior—the experience of middle age was always highly prized.

The men who drafted our Constitution stipulated in it that the President of the United States had to be at least 35 years old—but in fact, no one that young has ever been chosen by the people. The youngest president we have ever had, Theodore Roosevelt, was 42 when he took office; only six others were in their 40's when inaugurated, the youngest of them, John F. Kennedy, being 44 at the time and the others all over 45. And while the Constitution sets the minimum age for members of the House as low as 25 and for senators at a mere 30, even in our First Congress, when the nation was at its youngest, the average age of members of both houses was close to 45. In today's highly touted youth culture, Congress is even older than that: when the 93rd Congress convened in 1973, the average age of its members was 52 years (55.5 for senators, 51 for representatives), or about eight years older than the average for adult Americans.

What is true of Congress is true of most of our other major national institutions including courts, businesses, schools, and local governments. Our judges, business leaders, school superintendents and college administrators, village mayors and town councilmen, are nearly all people in their middle years. But this is not uniquely American; it is a general characteristic of modern industrial societies. As many sociologists have pointed out, in "traditional" societies it was the elders who held the power, but in most modern societies, power, wealth, and prestige tend to be concentrated among the middle-aged. Occasionally, some revolutionary government is headed chiefly by younger persons, as was originally the case in Castro's Cuba, but youth does not remain the essential criterion, and all too soon the revolution is run by the young who have become middle-aged, and later, as they grow really old, by their middle-aged successors.

What are we to make, then, of all the hullaballoo about the American youth culture? What are we to think of all the advertisements that tell us it's the young look that counts, the young tastes and ideas that are shaping our world? Are we to believe the prophets of only a few years ago who solemnly assured us that the hippie, blue-jeaned, beaded, loving, back-to-simplicity youth culture was taking over from the gray-haired, money-minded middle-aged, and leading to a "greening of America"?

Well, we have all benefited by some of the tastes and ideas lately introduced by the young, but the fact is that America is not a youth culture, and is not becoming one. It is a culture that prizes some of the values of youth, but simultaneously, and somewhat inconsistently, prizes even more highly most of the values of maturity and middle age. Of the whole vast accumulation of art, science, medicine, literature, language, custom, family life, and government that constitutes American culture, only a very small segment at the present moment (or at any time in the past) can be said to represent the special contribution of youth. Nor are the young of today dominating and reshaping our culture, despite the elegant exaggerations of such youth spokesmen as Theodore Roszak. We are influenced to some extent by their newest tastes in slang, music, and clothing, but these are relatively trivial and ephemeral fads; more importantly, we are absorbing some of their political values and their sexual liberalism—yet even these, seen in perspective, make up only a small part of the total American culture.

What properly deserves the name of youth culture, or, more accurately, youth subculture, is not American culture as such, but the particular values and the behavior of youth itself to the extent that it is differentiated from, and distinct from, the mainstream.

The important question is whether that subculture is what will become the culture of America's future, as the young grow older. The answer is no. Much of what youth is doing at any moment —flocking to hear a new kind of concert, experimenting with the latest drug or drink, meditating, or tilling the soil—is its way of dealing with the ambiguity, the uncertainty, the lack of power, of its social position. But after the school years, when the young begin to occupy real places in the social world, they have less and less need to define themselves as part of a distinct or rebellious subculture. And consequently, by the time they become the passers-on of culture to their children, what they pass on is the culture of American society and not the subculture of the youth group they once belonged to, though they may well retain and transmit a few elements of it.

Bernice L. Neugarten, professor of human development at the University of Chicago, has summed up the situation succinctly in *The Awareness of Middle Age:*

> Middle-aged men and women, while they by no means regard themselves as being in command of all they survey, nevertheless recognize that they constitute a powerful age group vis-à-vis other age groups; that they are the norm-bearers and the decision-makers; and that they live in a society which, while it may be oriented towards youth, is controlled by the middle-aged.

And while that may sound as if the middle-aged were a greedy, power-clutching group that dominates the young for selfish reasons, in actual fact the middle-aged control over society is in large part a useful, socially functional phenomenon, for the judgment of the middle-aged makes them the better operators and decision-makers of society. We hear, of course, that it is the middle-aged who have made the world the great mess it is, but this notion hardly stands up under analysis: the manifold dreadful problems of our time are the results of vast technological and political developments that not even middle age has had the wisdom to foresee and control, but for which youth is surely no sovereign remedy.

Even as radical a thinker as Simone de Beauvoir has recently said, in *The Coming of Age,* "One must have lived a long time to have a true idea of the human condition, and to have a broad view of the way in which things happen. . . . That is why, in the course of history, elderly men have been entrusted with great responsibilities."

But what comfort can those of us who are not senators, heads of banks, chairmen of boards, take from this? When it comes to the practical business of earning a living, are not most of us middle-aged people at a serious disadvantage? A number of the most visible careers in our country glorify the youth image until we who are middle-aged fear that if we lost our jobs we would find ourselves unwanted and unemployable. Many firms have always preferred young salespeople, most airlines have always hired young pretty stewardesses, office managers have generally put young receptionists out front, and in fast-moving high-pressure fields such as advertising and television, it is a commonplace that the bright young person with the hottest flame of ambition and latest gimmicky ideas has been the winner, while the experienced, solid, old hand is the loser.

More broadly, throughout American business there was, until very recently, a strong prejudice against the middle-aged job-seeker. Fifteen years ago, economist James R. Morris sent questionnaires to three hundred of the largest U.S. firms, asking about their hiring practices; over half replied, and nearly four out of ten of these admitted that they generally did not hire either hourly workers or salaried workers at age 50 or even less, and about a fifth generally did not hire salaried workers at age 45 or even less.

But in very recent years things have changed dramatically in this area of middle-aged life, as in so many others. Not only have unions grown ever more protective of the rights of their middle-aging members, but in 1967 the U.S. Congress passed the Age Discrimination in Employment Act, which went into effect in mid-1968 and is administered by the Employment Standard Administration of the Department of Labor. Essentially, the law prohibits employment discrimination against persons between the ages of 40 and 65. Physical or mental incompetence for the job, however, remains a valid reason for nonhiring or firing. Since 1968, many thousands of complaints of age discrimination have been dealt with by the E.S.A.; in fiscal 1973 alone, for instance, the agency took more than 7000 investigative actions, found age discrimination in over a third of these cases, and got compliance in nearly all of them, a small hard core of resisting employers having to be taken to court. The net result is that in the past few years the hiring and firing practices of American employers in regard to age have been undergoing a radical change, comparable to that being forced upon them in the areas of race and sex discrimination. Meanwhile, over two thirds of the states have enacted their own statutes and set up their own agencies to serve the same purpose.

Among the more visible results is the presence of middle-aging stewardesses on the airlines, but similar results exist in many another industry; in fiscal 1973 alone, E.S.A. actions opened up nearly 40,000 job opportunities of various sorts that had been illegally age-restricted, and an unknown but surely vast number of other job opportunities were opened up by employers who voluntarily complied with the law without having had to be forced to do so.

All in all, the employment-and-income picture for the middle-aged has become brighter than ever. Specifically:

—Middle age (as we said earlier) is now the peak earning period for both men and women in the labor force.

—For both sexes, it is the time of highest job stability, with very few middle-aged persons being fired or quitting, except to retire from work altogether.

—While many people at the upper end of the middle-age period do retire and go on Social Security, nearly all of those who choose to remain in the labor force are able to find or keep jobs. Unemployment among middle-aged males is actually lower than among young males, and shows only a slight increase beyond age 55; among females, the unemployment rate becomes lower and lower throughout life, up to age 64. This table tells the story:

1973 UNEMPLOYMENT RATES, SELECTED AGE GROUPS WITHIN THE LABOR FORCE *

Age	Males	Females
20–24	7.3%	8.4%
25–34	3.3%	5.8%
35–44	2.0%	3.9%
45–54	2.1%	3.2%
55–64	2.4%	2.8%

* Bureau of Labor Statistics: *Employment and Earnings,* vol. 20, no. 7, January 1974, p. 146.

While we have all heard a great deal about the difficulty of finding new employment if one loses or quits a job in middle age, in actual fact the average time it takes to find a new job is not much longer for the middle-aged than it is for young adults. In 1973, for instance, while men and women between 25 and 34 averaged somewhat over ten weeks of unemployment between jobs, those between 45 and 54 averaged only three weeks longer; even for those between 55 and 64, the average duration of unemployment was only six weeks longer than it was for the young. And encouraging as all this is, the figures for white-collar and highly skilled workers are even more so, their rates of unemployment being still lower and their time spent looking for new employment briefer.

The employers who have been forced to give the middle-aged an even break have lost little by it; indeed, in most cases they have gained. For a number of studies made for the Department of Labor show older workers in various occupations to be surprisingly productive, accurate, and reliable. Reflecting that surprise, sociologist Matilda White Riley observes in *Aging and Society,* "The older worker's greater experience on the job contributes to, but cannot entirely explain, his comparatively high output rates." What makes the difference is not solely experience on the job, but general life experience, resulting in commitment and good judgment rather than mere technical proficiency.

In terms of actual work output—whatever the unit of measurement used—the Department of Labor studies show only a minimal decline for employees of 45 and over, until age 65; the decline is particularly small in white-collar work, as compared to manual crafts. In studies of workers in occupations ranging from light industry to clerical work middle-aged workers had virtually the same output and degree of accuracy as younger ones, and in some areas they did even better. A study of 6000 federal mail sorters, for example, revealed that persons 45 to 49 sorted more consistently than those 35 to 44, and those 50 to 54 did still better; the 55-to-59 group dropped off a trifle (but was still above the 35-to-44 level), while the highest consistency level of all was that of sorters of 60 and over. Certain other surveys, cited by Dr. Morris, have reported that older workers in a steel mill and various light-industry plants were generally as productive as younger men, while those in retailing, clerical, and managerial work were actually more productive than their younger co-workers.

Other data collected by the Bureau of Labor Statistics of the Department of Labor reveal yet another facet of the middle-aged worker's good judgment: the rates of nondisabling injuries on the job are highest among 25- to 29-year-olds, and decline for each age group thereafter, reaching their lowest levels for workers in the 70- to-74 category. Surprisingly, too, older workers have lower absentee rates than younger ones, despite the generally better health of the young; apparently, those middle-aged and aging workers whose health is poor drop out of the labor force altogether, but those whose health is adequate and who remain at work are steadier and more reliable than the young.

These findings about the work capacity of the middle-aged apply not only to people doing repetitive or routine tasks, but to those in creative work as well. It is well known that in some fields—certain areas of science, in particular—young men often make highly original and important contributions, but in most creative fields the output of works reaches its highest level in the 40's or even later, the only known exception being among composers of chamber music. The evidence comes from Dr. Wayne Dennis, a professor of psychology at Brooklyn College, who compiled the percentages of works completed in each decade of life by 738 creative persons, all of whom lived to be at least 79. The figures are so remarkable that they deserve to be cited here in detail:

OUTPUT OF WORKS IN EACH DECADE OF LIFE, FOR SELECTED CREATIVE PROFESSIONALS IN PER CENTS OF TOTAL OUTPUT

Scholarship	20's	30's	40's	50's	60's	70's
Philosophers	3	17	20	18	22	20
Other scholars	6	17	21	21	16	19
Sciences						
Biologists	5	22	24	19	17	13
Botanists	4	15	22	22	22	15

	20's	30's	40's	50's	60's	70's
Chemists	11	21	24	19	12	13
Geologists	3	13	22	28	19	14
Inventors	2	10	17	18	32	21
Mathematicians	8	20	20	18	19	15

Arts

	20's	30's	40's	50's	60's	70's
Architects	7	24	29	25	10	4
Chamber musicians [composers]	15	21	17	20	18	9
Dramatists	10	27	29	21	9	3
Librettists	8	21	30	22	15	4
Novelists	5	19	18	28	23	7
Opera composers	8	30	31	16	10	5
Poets	11	21	25	16	16	10

To sum up:

—Middle-aged workers in manufacturing industries are very nearly as productive as younger workers, and generally more reliable and less given to absenteeism;

—Middle-aged clerical and white-collar workers range from nearly as productive and accurate as younger ones to definitely superior in both output and accuracy;

—Middle-aged scholars, scientists, writers, and other creative people are, generally, at the peak of their productivity in their 40's or later.

It is ironic that our society has so long been oversold on the superiority of youth in the world of work, and that business has, in consequence, discriminated against the middle-aged; it is a happy development for the middle-aged—and for our whole society—that this is now becoming a thing of the past. Unfortunately, for some time to come there will be a lag between law and custom, between the reality of middle-aged capabilities and the general recognition of that reality. There will still be needless tragedy in many lives.

Morton comments

This part of our discussion saddens me, for it reminds me of one of my dearest friends, whose story should be a cautionary tale for every middle-aged man. My friend Theodore W. had had a long and reasonably distinguished career in radio and television, first as a writer and interviewer on a New York news program, and later as an independent producer of a network show in the news field. He'd won awards, made good money, and become a familiar name in the business, but when he was 49, the sponsors of the show he was producing changed their advertising plans and dropped the show. Theodore, an independent, was out of a job. He started calling on network and station news heads and talent agents, but at the level he'd reached in his work there are relatively few positions, and at the time none was open. Having made his availability known everywhere, there was nothing he could do but wait.

I was seeing a lot of him then, and it was like being with a terminal cancer patient. Week by week he seemed to lose strength and to grow older. His face sagged, he sighed frequently, he grew round-shouldered. At the time, he was divorced, and had become engaged to a lovely woman, but he was so often silent or sullen that sometimes, in despair, she thought of calling it off; he himself suggested it a number of times, but they muddled on anyway. Summer came; he owned a tiny place at the seashore and retreated to it, but instead of swimming, sailing, gardening, or playing tennis, he lay immobilized on a deck chair with the phone beside him, drinking and smoking day after day and week after week, unable to leave the phone except for sheer physical necessities for fear the call of salvation would come through and he would miss it. (Urging him to get a telephone answering machine was of no avail; he said he *had* to be there when the call came.) Time and again, when we talked about his situation, he would tell me that he thought maybe the industry was right: it was the eager, bright, hyper-energetic young men with fresh ideas that were needed, not a person like himself—a has-been, a weary, burnt-out case.

And then one day, after half a year of waiting, the call came. Suddenly, Theodore was back in the thick of it as the co-producer of a major documentary series; he was brimming over with ideas, talking on three phones at once, turning out one fine special after another (and winning a national award for one of them), beginning a happy married life. But the story doesn't end happily, for during his long wait, when he was devoured by self-doubt, his heart had suffered (as hearts often do) from his profound emotional distress and total neglect of his health. He had had two minor coronary attacks during that period, but refused to be hospitalized for fear word would get around and wipe out whatever slim chances he had of getting another job. When he did get back to work, seemingly recovered but with some residual damage, his fear of ever being out of work again made him drive himself unmercifully, and in less than a year he had a third attack—this one massive and fatal.

I cannot be certain, but I have a very strong feeling that it was Theodore's dreadful loss of belief in himself, his acceptance of the mythology of middle age, that eroded his health during the long wait and eventually cut his life short at a time when the best two decades of it still lay ahead of him.

While experience, judgment, and commitment make the middle-aged person, in his work, anywhere from nearly as good as ever to better than ever, it is in the realm of human relationships that he has the clearest opportunities to live as a member of the privileged experience elite. For in our social relationships with fellow employees, spouses, sons and daughters, friends, neighbors, and the people we have business or community contacts with, we have a major advantage over the young: we have a sensitivity to what other people mean and to their needs, a sureness of our own feelings, a set of skills in human interaction, that can only come from a lifetime of learning.

This is exactly the opposite of the way the middle-aged are so often portrayed in cartoons, television comedies, and other forms of humor: they are shown as being stodgy, stuffy, out of touch with what's happening, unable to understand the young (or anyone different from themselves) or to grasp the subtleties of present-day life. There is some truth in this, but much untruth; the middle-aged *are* sometimes stubborn and persuaded of their own rightness—but in fact they do, a fair amount of the time, know better than the young. If they are so often made fun of, it is not because they are powerless fools but because, in fact, they are a powerful elite. Psychologists have often pointed out that a major function of humor is to vent the feelings of some part of society toward another part of which it is afraid: men long made jokes about women, whites about blacks, the laity about the clergy—and the young have long made fun of the middle-aged and still do. But we who are middle-aged can take a perverse satisfaction in this: the very mockery of middle age is a tribute to its social position.

No wonder the young resent the middle-aged. Young people not only haven't yet learned how to deal with many problems in human relationships, they haven't yet become aware of what most of those problems are. And they know it. The middle-aged, on the other hand, do have a general awareness of most of the problems in human relationships, a capacity to perceive and interpret meanings in words and behavior, an ability to make essential discriminations among those meanings and to be appropriately compassionate—or appropriately critical; above all, they have the self-assurance that they can cope easily and effectively with almost any situation they encounter.

These are general terms; let's be specific. Can you remember how, as a young person, you suffered when you had to walk alone into a roomful of people, particularly if most of them were strangers to you? Or when you couldn't think of anything interesting to say to someone attractive you had just met, or someone you were dating for the first time? Can you recall how hideously embarrassing it was when you had to walk into a store and ask the manager for a summer job? Or tell a professor that you thought he had made an error in grading your exam? Or ask your boss for a raise? Or ask a friend if it was true that he'd made some derogatory remarks about you to someone else? Or tell someone you'd been seeing regularly that it wasn't working out and that you wanted to be free to see others?

What made these and innumerable other situations so agonizing when you were young was that you simply lacked experience: you did not know exactly how to speak or act in the situation, you did not know how to predict the other person's responses, you could not anticipate how you would react to those unpredictable responses, you did not know whether you would be unnerved, inept, speechless, helpless, or whether you would manage to deal with the situation effectively.

Living with uncertainty and alarm is intolerable; to endure, the organism must learn to deal with situations easily and efficiently. This is the meaning of becoming experienced at living. Sociologist Erving Goffman illustrates the process by means of extreme examples: "When we examine the activity of a practiced pilot, sword swallower, skier, snake-handler, or bomb defuser it is perfectly plain that his capacity to be at ease with his activity now was preceded by a period, often quite long, when catastrophe seemed everywhere and his attention had to be completely given over to saving his skin." But, he says, through a long process of learning and training, the individual becomes capable of swiftly and surely appraising situations, and hence of dealing with them without undue effort. "The individual's ease in a situation," Goffman adds, "presumes that he has built up experience in coping with the threats and opportunities occurring within the situation. He acquires a survivably short reaction time—the period needed to sense alarm, to decide on a correct response, and to respond. And as a result, he has not so much come to know the world around him as he has become experienced and practiced in coping with it."

All of which is as true of social relationships as it is of piloting a plane or defusing a bomb. Through long training, we become capable of sensing the potentialities in any social encounter, calculating the probable outcomes of various actions on our part, making the most suitable choice, and acting upon it—all within a workably brief time, often within a split second. The most important period of this training is that which follows upon our leaving the familial nest and making our own way in society; it is not surprising, therefore, that this kind of competence and ease is rare in people in their 20's, begins to appear in those in their 30's, and is, finally, common in those in their 40's and beyond. Psychologist Robert F. Peck, delivering a paper on "The Psychological Aspects of Aging" at an American Psychological Association conference, suggested that "wisdom" seems to be a word used to sum up an increment in judgment through sheer experience. It is to be distinguished from intellectual capacity, Peck said, and might be defined as the ability to make the most effective choices; while choice-making is subject to various influences, "Sheer life experience seems to be essential in giving one a chance to encounter a wide range of emotional relationships, as a corrective to the overgeneralized perceptual-attitudinal set derived from one's necessarily limited experience in one family, and one subculture, during childhood and adolescence."

The enlarging of our life experience in young adulthood—an educational process which seems to take just about as long as the entire process of arriving at adulthood in the first place—yields, finally, a sense of *mastery* over our environment, according to Professor Neugarten. From a depth study of one hundred middle-aged university and professional people, published under the title "The Awareness of Middle Age," she concluded:

> Despite the new realization of the finiteness of time, one of the most prevailing themes expressed by these middle-aged respondents is that middle adulthood is the period of maximum capacity and ability to handle a highly complex environment and a highly differentiated self. Very few express a wish to be young again. . . . We have been impressed with the central importance of what might be called the executive processes of personality in middle age: self-awareness, selectivity, manipulation and control of the environment, mastery, competence, the wide array of cognitive strategies. . . . These people feel that they effectively manipulate their social environments on the basis of prestige and expertise; and that they create many of their own rules and norms. There is a sense of increased control over impulse life. The successful middle-aged person often describes himself as no longer "driven," but as now the "driver"—in short, "in command."

All of which yields what may be the ultimate gratification of middle age: self-approval. For as the late Abraham Maslow and various other psychologists have shown, the ability to deal effectively with one's environment (including the people in it) and to exercise control or influence is a prime source of self-esteem. When we know what to expect of other people, and possess the skills of dealing effectively with our social environment, we approve of ourselves—and this is a consummation we have devoutly wished for ever since, as children, we sought the approval of the adults in our lives. And now that, finally, we are the adults in our own lives, we have found the final answer to be self-approval.

The sense of mastery, the achievement of ease in dealing with the social world, has yet another and very special reward: it brings us a new and wonderfully satisfying role—that of teacher and adviser. In other societies, as we said earlier, it was the aged who were the seers, the counselors, the decision-makers; in our own society, the middle-aged hold this distinguished and important place. Not in a formalized way, to be sure; yet it is undeniable that for all the emphasis on and admiration of youthfulness, the social expertise gained during two or more decades of adult life earns the middle-aged the somewhat grudging respect of younger people. They turn, from time to time, to the middle-aged—not only the famous among them, but to all those, says Dr. Peck, who are informally recognized to be mature and experienced—for counsel, advice, reassurance. This aspect of the relationships between the young and the middle-aged has been underplayed in recent years —almost conducted furtively, but with middle age now coming into its own, this is beginning to change.

We two, the authors of this book, often turned to experienced and wise friends for advice and assistance when we were younger, and even did so only a handful of years ago when we were both between marriages and, in our different ways, at a loss. More recently, we have in turn been deeply gratified that friends of all ages sometimes seek us out when they are temporarily in need of our particular experience; they confide in us and ask for our opinions, have us listen and help them think through their own half-formed thoughts about a personal problem. We both try to avoid acting like pundits or authorities at such times, but individually and collectively we *have* had a good deal of life experience and learned a fair amount from it; we can, therefore, listen to almost anything a friend tells us without shock, revulsion, or criticism, and can often ask the questions or offer the personal reactions that make the friend search his own mind and feelings and come, at last, to his own decision.

The opportunity to perform this role for a friend is deeply

gratifying if it proves to be helpful. But perhaps most gratifying of all is the chance to share one's experience and judgment with one's own grown children. When they were small, we were, in their eyes, the most wonderful people on earth—all-knowing, all-powerful, flawless. But then they began to grow up, and almost immediately after they had passed through the "Would-you-please-help-me-with-my-math" phase (and found that sometimes we couldn't), there came a time when we wondered why our children had so little respect for our intelligence, our accomplishments, and our human experience—and so much more respect for those of nearly every other adult. But they were becoming their own persons and had to separate themselves from us before they could, for the first time, see us objectively as human beings.

But how extraordinary, how fulfilling it is, when one magical day your own child, now an independent adult, comes to you with a question about some problem, asks for your advice or help, wants to draw upon your experience and your judgment. It may be only about some mundane and practical matter (how and when to put in the tomato plants; what kind of household insurance to carry); it may be about some more complex and difficult interpersonal matter (how to deal with a hostile or troublesome neighbor); it may even be about how to deal with an ultimate life problem (how to handle one's feelings about the impending death of a relative or friend). But at any level, there is something very special and wonderfully satisfying about being able to give what is asked out of your store of experience and wisdom.

Bernice comments

A few years ago, my first grandchild was born. My daughter and son-in-law were planning on natural childbirth, breast-feeding, everything as close to nature as possible, and such a plan did not call for any strangers in the household. Would I, they asked, spend a week or so with them after the baby was born, to lend a hand and to help them learn to differentiate between a hungry cry, a sleepy cry, or a cry of pain? With a sense of panic, I realized that it was more than twenty years since my own last infant had been born, and it was entirely possible that I had lost my ear and my touch. But of course I said that

I would be delighted and—I think—managed not to communicate my anxiety at all, but only my very real pleasure.

As things worked out, both mother and father did a grand job with the breathing and panting maneuvers, and Elizabeth was born so quickly, easily, and happily that she came home from the hospital when she was two and a half days old. And there was Grandma on the job.

To my amazement, I found that I was an instant old pro; I could have been handling infants all my life. My chief responsibility was to keep the baby with me during the night so that her mother could get some rest. Every time she awakened to be fed (which was *very* often), I changed her and carried her into her mother's room. During the day, I was *asked*, mind you, to demonstrate such bits of esoterica as how to give a bath, put on an undershirt without creating trauma, elicit a burp. By the time my lessons ended, I felt urgently in need of a good night's sleep—but much more important, I felt needed, useful, loved, happy. Years of my own life experience made that week possible and my experience was still accumulating as I learned to be a grandmother.

Morton comments

In one capacity or another, I've taught, given advice to, and been consulted by many people about many things, and have often been pleased by what I was able to do. But nothing has been as meaningful to me as an event of only a few months ago. My son Jeff, then a freshman at Vassar, came to visit us during his spring vacation, and almost at once brought up the subject of his biggest current worry —his need to decide by next year on his major subject, and, by implication, his probable career and whole future. He said that this was the thing that was really troubling him—and then, a trifle hesitantly, added that he hoped I might be able to help him with it.

I hadn't felt so glad and proud since the moment the doctor walked into the hospital room where I was waiting, nearly nineteen years earlier, and informed me that I had just become the father of a fine baby boy. I told Jeff I'd be very happy to talk to him about it, in good time; then, for the next several days, I asked a lot of questions, paid close attention when he discussed anything and everything with

Bernice and with visitors, and listened to him as if I had never listened to him before. And one morning after he and I had played two hard sets of tennis, I invited him to sit down with me in my study and have a look at the problem.

I won't go into the details here; they're immaterial, and in any case they're Jeff's private business. But in general, we talked about the kinds of things he has enjoyed, those he has been particularly good at, those he liked but was less good at; we speculated about the various goals one can have in life, the purposes of work, the rewards and costs of various kinds of success; we weighed his desire to make an early choice against the dangers of choosing too soon, before he knew enough about himself (at which point I told him about my own two mistakes in career choice, and my subsequent corrections of those choices). We talked a good deal, too, about sex and love, and about marriage and friendship, about the kinds of life plans that would make ample room for these things, and about other kinds of plans that left little or no room for them.

When we were all through, Jeff seemed immensely relieved and cheered. There were more possibilities ahead than he had realized; more than that, important things he had felt and believed (but not known he had felt and believed) had come to the surface. He had some basis now for his next year's plans, and a general but thoroughly flexible view of his long-range future. He had arrived at conclusions he had been ready to reach but had not known how to reach by himself, and now he had done so partly by using his own resources, partly by drawing upon my experience and judgment.

I felt, at the end of that discussion, that I had given him more than I had in all the years of paying bills and buying gifts. But most wonderfully, I felt that I myself had been given something price-less—the reward of his seeing me as a man of wisdom.

Finally, we want to say something about the role of experience in that area of human behavior in which it has been the most undervalued, and yet is perhaps the most important: namely, love. We're not referring here to sexual expertise, though there's no doubt that experience and skill count for a great deal in sexual behavior. We mean, rather, the total emotional relationship between a man and a woman.

Throughout the ages, literature has celebrated and glorified the beauty and intensity of young love: Hero and Leander, Tristan and Iseult, Romeo and Juliet, were all very young, and all were experiencing the rapture of love for the first time. And it has always been the stories of such loves that have captivated us and moved us to tears. Why tears?—because as unbearably sweet and transfiguring as young love is, in literature it almost always ends in tragic death. Not because that's how things are in real life, but because first love is so often part illusion, part fantasy, that it does not last; as experience makes the lovers aware of reality, their love loses its glory, fades, even turns to bitterness. The lovers live, but their love dies; poets and dramatists make the story more satisfying by having the lovers die and their love live on.

We do not die, but learn from our early love experiences; we find out something about ourselves and about the kind of mate we need and the kind that might need us; we find out both the rewards and the shortcomings of one kind of interaction, and begin to anticipate the possibilities of other kinds. Generally we choose a little better the next time, and the next, coming ever closer to loving on the basis of reality rather than imagined perfection. We become ever more adept at picking up clues to a partner's moods and needs, more adept at communicating our own moods and needs rather than hiding them behind a façade. We begin to experience love as, in part, the giving of ourselves to the other, and not solely as winning the other's person and affection.

In their first loves, young lovers know little of all this; how could they? A very few couples do eventually learn it with each other—a very few, that is, have their first love last a lifetime, growing and maturing through trial and error, exploration and growth. But most people require a number of different love experiences, each adding something to their store of knowledge and maturity, before they have that essential minimum of emotional expertise to make a genuine commitment. Various surveys, for instance, suggest that most young college-level men and women have about six to ten more or less important love relationships between adolescence and marriage. But people who marry very young, without such a series of learning experiences, have a very much greater chance of divorce than those who take longer and learn more about themselves and about love before marrying.

Yet even years of trial-and-error learning do not make most

young married persons fully qualified members of the experience elite as far as love is concerned. In some areas of the marriage relationship, marital adjustment—a dull-sounding word for something beautiful and precious—takes many months; in other areas it takes years. And a large proportion of those who marry never do acquire the knowledge and maturity to reach a high level of marital adjustment, or they fail to keep pace in their love relationship with other changes in their lives. In cold numerical terms, there are now roughly one third as many divorces as marriages each year; one can regard that as a measure of the incidence of inexperience and lack of expertise in the primary social relationship we call love.

Cynics claim that the high and still climbing divorce rate proves that marriage is bankrupt and obsolete as an institution. Rubbish! Marriage is more popular than ever; even though a growing number of young single people delay marrying for a while, in actual statistical fact the percentages of adults who have ever married or who are currently married are higher in nearly every age group than they were at the turn of the century, in the supposed heyday of marriage. But the nature of marriage, and our expectations of it, have changed dramatically; we now expect emotional fulfillment rather than practical and social benefits, and lacking such fulfillment we divorce, test out new relationships—and usually, sooner or later, remarry.

But what of the first marriages that do last for life? They are still in the majority; what has become of them by middle age—have they become better through life experience? We've already said that, by and large, marriages that last until middle age become, on the average, more satisfactory in that period of life than they have been for most of the previous fifteen or twenty years. In part, that's due to all those practical advantages of postparental life of which we have spoken so much; but in part it's due to the accumulation of experience as a partnership—to expertise in the married interaction that is acquired slowly, as is expertise in every other social relationship.

Yet marriage is not like any other social relationship; because it is so tightly bound by custom and social expectations, many people remain in defective marriages without learning or improving the relationship, but rather by falling into defensive habits. People learn all sorts of avoidance techniques; what is worse, they learn to take "revenge" in subtle or overt ways, their behavior becoming not unlike that of two hostile neighboring countries that dare not make real war against other, but periodically engage in border skirmishes to leak off some of their pent-up anger.

We are all familiar with such "frozen marriages"—relationships that have become congealed in a pattern of mingled love and hate, or "antagonistic cooperation," as it is sometimes called; marriages whose participants long ago ceased to learn from experience, stopped improving their coping mechanisms, and have merely gone on repeating their imperfect pattern of interaction. There are many such patterns described in the technical literature, but one example, drawn from our own experience, will serve as an illustration. Both of us have known Jeremy and Peggy G. for some years, and both of us are very fond of them; unhappily, neither of us is at all fond of their interaction with each other. They live in another city and we don't see them very often, but whenever we do, we have a grand time together for a while; then, inevitably, the conversation takes a turn something like this (Jeremy, it's important to note, is a physician, and Peggy used to be a nurse):

Morton: Did you see that fascinating piece in today's paper about the new heart studies?

Peggy: I noticed it, but you *know* I wouldn't read it. There isn't anything that interests me less than medicine; that's why I got out of nursing.

Jeremy: It *was* fascinating and really significant. Actually, I had read about it a few days ago in one of the journals and—

Peggy: Hey, have you two seen the new Woody Allen movie? I've heard it's marvelous and I'm just dying to see it, but I guess I'll have to go alone. You know how Jeremy is, he never seems to have time to do anything *I* want to do.

Bernice: Yes, we saw it on our last trip to city and loved it. It's even funnier than the one we all saw together.

Peggy: I guess I'll try to see it next week. It's too bad that Jeremy doesn't enjoy anything except his work.

Peggy speaks in a sweet and gentle voice, while faintly smiling; she looks at her husband lovingly and indulgently all the time she is talking and she has told us many times how much she adores him. And no doubt, she really believes she does. But in only three brief statements she managed to convey (1) that she has no interest whatsoever in Jeremy's work, (2) that she has little respect for him as a person since she interrupted the moment he began to say something, (3) that Jeremy is selfish and never considers his wife's desires, and (4) that he's a dull fellow and a spoilsport who doesn't enjoy doing anything for fun.

We used to feel sorry for Jeremy, an intelligent, enthusiastic, and kindly man whom we invariably find interesting and pleasant to be with. But eventually, we concluded that he is as much to blame as his wife for the faults in their relationship and for their failure to learn from their innumerable experiences with each other. If Jeremy's opinion of himself were better than it is, he would confront Peggy with her ill-concealed hostility; he would insist on their examining it together, so as to understand it and to change whatever it is that causes it. Instead, he accepts each attack with an apologetic smile. While a public confrontation would not be in order, it is quite clear from the unchanging nature of the relationship that there has never been a private one; Jeremy grows ever more meek, quietly ignores Peggy's fire, and goes his own way—possibly using the situation as a justification for immersing himself in his work more and more.

Just as many a run-of-the-mill tennis player has faulty habits he isn't aware of and therefore may play for a lifetime without getting any better, so many married couples have flaws in their interaction which they themselves fail to perceive and hence are unable to correct. In order to learn from experience and to improve their relationship, like tennis players they need help from a "pro"—a professional marriage counselor or psychotherapist who might enable them to see and to understand what they are doing, and to begin to test out new and different ways of responding to each other. Actually, the success ratio of marriage counseling is nothing to cheer about; a recent survey suggests that of couples who jointly seek such help, only about half of those married less than twelve years, and only a little over a third of those married longer, receive definite benefit from it. But even that is far better than the proportion of frozen marriages that improve spontaneously.

Joint marriage counseling isn't the only answer, of course. If either partner is reluctant to take part in it, the other one can seek help alone to cope with his or her emotions, and any growth of unilateral understanding is bound to produce change in the marriage. The marriage may well improve; it may also deteriorate and dissolve—an outcome we personally consider preferable to the frozen condition in which neither partner can possibly be happy.

If Peggy, for instance, were to go into psychotherapy without Jeremy's participation, sooner or later she would be certain to discover the extent of her (perhaps unconscious) hostility toward Jeremy. She would begin to ask herself whether it stems from jealousy of his eminence and her lack of it—in which case she might decide to go back to work for her ego's sake instead of just being the doctor's wife. Or, she might find that her anger was left over from some old unforgiven hurt which she had concealed beneath her other complaints—in which case she might finally confront him with it and work it out for once and for all. On the other hand, she might discover that her hostility has nothing to do with Jeremy at all, but is a carryover of her childhood feelings toward her father, her brother, or some other man important in her life.

If Jeremy, conversely, were the one who went into individual therapy, he would surely have to confront himself, in time, with the fact that he has never made any creative effort either to change or to challenge Peggy's behavior, but has always just accepted it. He would have to ask himself whether he is afraid to incur her anger, and if so, whether that fear is an unreasonable leftover from his own childhood. Or he might explore whether or not he has any real or imagined reasons for feeling guilty (does he, for example, think he is deficient in giving warmth?) and therefore accepts continual minor punishment as only proper. These are just some of the things he might learn that would change his life.

What percentage of middle-aged marriages are frozen and have never fully developed, there is no way of knowing. But although such marriages catch the attention and therefore seem numerous, the weight of evidence, much of which we have cited earlier, suggests that they are in the minority. Most marriages either survive because the partners adapt to and profit from their experience as a couple, or wither away and break up.

Similarly, love relationships with others outside the marriage can be important or even profound learning experiences—or can be merely diversions and amusements, without significant value for the individual or the marriage. In an earlier chapter, we said that extramarital relationships, though they may sometimes be temporarily useful, are not a viable way of life for the great majority of the middle-aged. Here, we want to focus our attention on extramarital acts as a type of learning experience, for whatever else they do, they add to the individual's accumulation of experience, altering his perceptions of his needs and goals—and thereby modifying his behavior. According to the 1972 survey, by early middle age nearly half of all married men and nearly one fifth of all married women have had such experiences. Their marriages—and divorces—are in part a reflection of what they learned, in those experiences, about themselves, their spouses, and the worth or worthlessness of outside relationships.

In most marriages that remain intact despite extramarital activity by one or both partners, such activity is kept secret; nonetheless, it almost always changes not only the one who has it but the spouse as well. Sometimes, for instance, it makes the unfaithful partner aware of sexual and emotional possibilities that he or she had never explored with the spouse, and which he or she now introduces into the marital relationship, to its benefit. Kinsey and certain others thought that this was a frequent outcome of secret extramarital experience; Morton's own surveys (see his 1969 and 1974 books) make us think that improvement of the marital sexual or emotional relationship occurs in only a small minority of the cases.

But marriage often benefits indirectly, in quite another way, from the unfaithful partner's learning experience. For in a large number of cases, the one who has secret extramarital relationships learns, after a while, that the exhilaration and excitement such activity provides are outweighed by the inner conflict, fear of discovery, and emotional stress it causes. Accordingly, most of these people have only a limited period of extramarital activity, after which they return (as secretly as they left) to a state of faithful monogamy, enlightened and experienced about the rewards and the costs of extramarital affairs. To that extent, the marriage may be the better for it; the fantasy has been tested out and found not worth the price.

A number of people—a minority, to judge from the reports, but a substantial minority—do discover that extramarital involvements enrich their lives and compensate for shortcomings of the marriage when, for various reasons, they can neither improve their marriages nor abandon them. They want the combination of a cool, relatively distant marital relationship and the excitement of secret, passionate meetings with a mistress or lover. Sociologist John Cuber and others have found this pattern to be preferred by, and feasible for, people whose marriages are essentially "utilitarian"—practical, businesslike, and not very intimate. On the basis of our own interviews and research, we suggest that this adaptation occurs most often in those who are uncomfortable in or cannot tolerate at all a totally intimate relationship, and who therefore function better in two or more partial or segmental relationships. While this obviously is not what we've been plumping for throughout this book, if it best meets the needs of any individual and does not frustrate the needs of his or her spouse, it can be considered a successful mode of coping with the emotional-sexual side of life and a valid outcome of experience.

So much for secret extramarital activity. But what of extramarital activity that becomes known to the other spouse? What kind of change does that experience produce in that other spouse and in the marriage? We are not speaking here of mutually permitted extramarital behavior, a subject we mentioned in Chapter 4, but of secret extramarital behavior that comes to light in one way or another and violates the expectations of the deceived partner.

Its first effect, even in this supposedly liberated era, is nearly always to create intense turmoil. The experience, for the one who has been deceived, is one of betrayal and abandonment, and results in enormous hurt and rage; the reaction to being exposed, on the part of the one who has been unfaithful, is either one of guilt and self-abasement or, conversely, of defiance and self-justification. The struggle and the suffering of the two partners is often as severe as any they have ever known or ever will know. In a fair number of cases, the net result of the experience for both partners is to make the marriage seem intolerable; some marriages break up at once, some only after a lingering death. But the number that are actually broken by extramarital activity can easily be exaggerated; infidelity is said to be implicated in about a third of all divorces, but in many of these the extramarital activity was the result of discontents or conflicts that would have brought the marriage to an end anyway.

A good deal more often, if the extramarital activity was not a product of anger or frustration and if the marriage is fundamentally viable, it survives. The partners generally go through an agonizing period of struggle, recrimination, and emotional exhaustion. Sometimes they merely "patch up" their differences, agreeing that there will be no further episodes and no further discussion of the past ones; needless to say, this is a poor solution, because the unresolved angers come out in other forms and continue to do so for many years.

Other people discuss the problem more earnestly and searchingly, and end by resolving it. Sometimes they recognize that the infidelity was a transient phenomenon produced by outside forces such as anxiety over fading youth, a period of stress on the job, or an unavoidable separation, and thereupon dismiss it as having had no real significance. Sometimes the partners search for, and find, deeper sources of dissatisfaction or conflict that led to the infidelity, and set about mending them. In either case, it is a genuine learning experience for both parties; despite the stress and the pain they have endured, they are the richer for it—not in the sense that their love has become deeper or more joyous, but in the sense that each of them has become more understanding and mature.

And maturity, whether arrived at by this means or by less painful ones, is the *summum bonum*, the highest good, to be gained from forty or more years of experience. When each partner in a love relationship is truly mature, each seeks to do for the other what he most desires the other to do for him—sense his needs and respond to them, anticipate his anxieties and forestall them. The late Harry Stack Sullivan, one of the most original minds in American psychiatry, said it about as well as it can ever be said:

The last of these great developments [of the mature personality] is the ... need for intimacy—for collaboration ... and in this collaboration there is the very striking feature of a very lively sensitivity to the needs of the other and to the interpersonal security or absence of anxiety in the other.

You might well copy that out, underline it in red, and hang it by the marital bedside, as the first and greatest commandment concerning married love. As we ourselves did—removing it from the wall only when, at last, we felt that it had become an ineradicable part of us.

6 *The Midcourse Correction*

TAKING A NEW LOOK AT
OURSELVES AT MID-LIFE AND
MAKING ADJUSTMENTS ACCORDING
TO OUR NEW PERCEPTIONS

The New Middle Age has arrived at roughly the same moment in history as space travel; it is therefore wonderfully appropriate that one of the most familiar concepts of space technology—the midcourse correction—should also be applicable to middle age and to some of the most significant steps in making it the Prime Time of life.

The term, in rocketry, applies to certain corrective maneuvers that have to be made at a point between the end of the powered flight and the beginning of the reentry phase. As applied to middle age, midcourse correction refers to those changes that must be made early in mid-life—that point in the passage through life when the trajectory that has been suitable so far is about to carry us off course. We have, naturally, been making minor semiautomatic adjustments all along, such as changing jobs, buying larger houses, and learning to deal with our growing children. But with the advent of middle age, our whole life situation changes dramatically in the many ways that have been discussed thus far, and a more conscious reappraisal of the self and modification of life-style is called for. This runs the gamut from the way we dress to the company we keep, and from our attitudes toward work and play to those toward birth and death.

All of which is implied in our use of the term midcourse correction. Some of the adjustments we are about to suggest may seem familiar, and easy to achieve; others—the more important ones—

may seem bizarre or radical, and difficult or impossible to carry out. Yet the most difficult thing about any of them is not their actual execution, but rather managing in the first place to take a clear, fresh look at ourselves, to reconsider, to reappraise. What follows, therefore, is not so much a set of specific recommendations as an effort to get you, the reader, to think about each of a number of areas of your life in which change may be necessary; having done so, you—better than anyone else—can then calculate the midcourse correction called for in your own case.

A familiar and obvious area for correction is that of general *comportment*—the individual's mode of dress and speech, his mannerisms, and his overall style of interacting with other people. The words, gestures, clothing, and public personality that were right for someone at 20 or 25 are bound to be wrong at 45 or 50; they express a bygone self, not the present one. They are inappropriate, disturbing to others, and do not in any way *work.* Yet many people cling to outmoded patterns, oblivious to their inappropriateness but baffled by a growing sense of personal failure.

Jennifer W. is a case in point. She and her husband, Tony, were married twenty-four years ago, shortly after they both graduated from college. It had been a glorious senior year for Jennifer—she had been the prom queen and one of the most popular students on campus with both men and women. Jennifer was not only pretty—a willowy blonde with a sparkling smile, dimples, and a doll-like face—but she was sunshiny, happy-go-lucky, friendly, and ingenuous. Far from being a sexy *femme fatale,* she was laughingly and ever so slightly flirtatious with men, and warm and outgoing with women. While she had never been a particularly good student, her winning personality as well as her good looks charmed her professors into keeping her at a safe C average.

When her engagement to Tony was announced, there were several deeply grieved young men in her circle, but even they had to admit that it was an ideal match. Tony was tall and good-looking, and a dean's list student whose high grades seemed to come to him without effort. He always had time for socializing and was as full of fun and high spirits as Jennifer. No matter what the pair did, they always seemed to be having a gayer and better time than anyone else and they were often likened to Zelda and Scott Fitzgerald in the golden years of that famous couple's life.

Tony and Jennifer are in their upper 40's now. Tony is still handsome, though a trifle heavy, but the gray at his temples and his elegant, conservative way of dressing make him look like the successful and distinguished economist he is. No longer boyish and devil-may-care, he is now urbane and almost courtly but still conveys a sense of genuine warmth and a twinkling wit.

Jennifer, on the other hand, still tries to look and act just like the prom queen she was in her senior year. Although she has grown a trifle thick-waisted and somewhat heavy of bosom, she continues to wear her blond hair loose and shoulder-length, and to fling it about with girlish insouciance. Her face is still doll-like (with the help of a thick mask of cosmetics) and she still favors flouncy, girlish dresses similar to the ones she seemed so adorable in long ago. In company, and even at home, she giggles easily, flashes her bewitching smile while batting her eyelashes, and even uses a bit of baby talk now and then. At a party, she is apt to impulsively clap her hands and announce some grand idea for a new game, a midnight swim, or a mass descent, champagne in hand, upon some stodgy neighbor.

But alas, her girlish charm has lost its old magic. At home, Tony tends to look bored and weary rather than delighted and loving when Jennifer switches her hair around, makes a pouting face, and plumps herself down on his lap to wheedle him into changing his mind about something. At parties, the old charm is even less successful: the men whose eyes used to follow her whenever she entered a room now hardly notice her. Of late, she has been aware that when she draws one of them into conversation, he is apt to look restless and distracted rather than intrigued and titillated as of yore, and to quickly find some excuse to drift off. In an effort to turn the tide, she has grown more and more seductive.

Jennifer suspects that the men are not really to blame for their cold behavior but rather that their wives have been plotting against her. She can't imagine what has gone wrong, but there is no doubt that these women, her dear friends, have been avoiding her of late; she knows of several occasions when they went into the city to attend a matinee or visit a museum and did not ask her to join them. Poor Jennifer is deeply hurt but she really doesn't understand what the trouble is.

Tony does, but he doesn't know what to do about it. He recognizes that while everyone else in their group has gradually taken on a mature identity, Jennifer is still enacting the role of an enchanting college student of the late 1940's. He realizes that their friends are bored with her for she has nothing to contribute to their conversations or their lives. She has clung steadfastly to a self that is grossly unsuitable in one who has been an adult for so many years, instead of evolving and growing in accordance with her life experiences. Though Tony often feels embarrassed by the way Jennifer looks and acts, he has not found any way to change her. On a few occasions, when he suggested that she might look marvelous with her hair done in a chignon, or cut to a shorter length, she instantly and firmly said, "But it wouldn't be *me!*" Once, he bought her a handsome and expensive Italian knit dress for her birthday; she kissed him warmly and said she hoped his feelings wouldn't be hurt but although the dress was lovely, it didn't suit her at all. The next day she exchanged it for two of the ruffly little dresses she preferred. Occasionally Tony has tried to talk to Jennifer about acting less cute, flirtatious, or girlishly irrepressible, but either she didn't understand what he was talking about or she became so hurt and tearful that he lost the courage to try again.

Not only do Tony's friends no longer envy him as they once did, but now *he* is often aware of envying *them*. He feels genuinely wistful when he hears their wives take part intelligently and earnestly in some interesting discussion, and he finds himself admiring some of those wives for their poise and womanliness. He thinks that Jennifer's suspicion is well founded—the other women *are* avoiding her—and he suspects that their friends invite the two of them only out of loyalty to him. Sometimes he wonders how long that loyalty will last.

Nearly everybody knows at least one person who, like Jennifer, clings to a formerly successful but now outgrown self. There are many variations—the former college athlete who still plays the big jock; the helpless kid (or Poor Soul), forever begging friends to help him or her out of some emotional or practical crisis; the young innocent (or perennial novice), always listening, wide-eyed and admiring; and so forth. Yet it is as natural and inevitable as gravity that every living thing must change as time goes by. The error of those who cling to an outgrown self is that they view all change in terms of loss rather than gain, and therefore seek to shun, deny, or ignore it.

But change is not necessarily loss, not even in the area of physical appearance. The middle-aged, though they may not have the smooth flesh or luxuriant hair of youth, have their own special potential for physical appeal, and can make the most of it by being true to themselves. We all owe it to ourselves, our mates, and even our friends to stay as attractive as possible. We should make use of diet, exercise, flattering clothing, becoming makeup, and the use of hair color if we like it and it is natural-looking. But any effort at enhancing our appearance succeeds only if we carry it out in a way suited to our real, present selves and not in a way suited to the very young. A girlish dress and hairstyle only make a middle-aged woman's face and figure look older, but a more adult dress and hairstyle complement her ripe appeal. The 50-year-old man stuffed into too-tight hip-huggers, with his shirt open to the waist displaying tufts of gray hair, and with the sparse hair on his head combed forward over his forehead, looks either too fat, withered, or just plain ludicrous. The same man in up-to-date but not extreme sport clothes, and with his hair combed in a normal fashion—even if it lets the thin spots show—has a mature manliness and is actually more youthful-looking than the aging college-boy type.

Morton comments

What we've been saying about physical appearance applies as well to physical activities. Ten years ago, I was very keen on a whole round of *mucho macho* sports—cruising in a sailboat, flying a single-engine plane, learning to jump hurdles in a riding academy—all of which seemed to me exciting and rewarding. And indeed such activities are, but now, with the perspective of hindsight, I think that I valued them not so much for themselves as for making me feel that I was still young, and for enabling me to broadcast that image of myself. In the last few years, I've rethought the matter and made some changes. I still love flying in small planes, but I don't do the piloting any longer because I haven't the time to keep up my skills, and it's damned foolishness to fly at all if you don't fly enough to be expert at it. So I've quit, and if anyone thinks that that means I'm older and wiser, they're right. I've also stopped riding horses, and have limited my sailing to fooling around in a little lateen-rigged dinghy, because I have so many other compelling leisure interests now that are more compatible with my present way of life. At least two of them, tennis and gardening, are even better than riding or sailing for keeping my middle-aged body in condition, and I find them more relaxing. I may not be able to make myself sound quite as dashing as formerly, but I'm pleased to say that I don't seem to need to any longer.

If the physical changes that come with time need not be seen only as loss, those that take place in one's personality and behavior can—and should—be seen as great gain. To continue to play the same part and project the same self as when we were young is to cheat ourselves and our associates of all that we have been and become over the years. For after a quarter of a century of adult life we should be vastly richer and more valuable as personalities. We have read innumerable books, seen countless movies and plays, traveled to many places, listened to a multitude of musical perform-ances; we have loved in many ways and perhaps loved many people, had many friends and perhaps a few enemies, shared joys and griefs with others, helped our children grow, lived in different homes, worked at various kinds of jobs. We have known illness, been touched by death. How could we possibly have remained the same? We *must* be different. To make our midcourse correction, we need to submit to the most scrupulous self-examination to find out who we are *now*. How do we see ourselves? And how do others appraise us? A large part of our feelings about ourselves is a reflec-tion of what we perceive in the attitudes of others. If people respect and admire us, we will have a sense of self-esteem. And if this is the case, we can be fairly sure that our behavior, unlike Jennifer's, is appropriate to the present. We are mature adults and should take pride and pleasure in the security that comes with firmly asserting our middle-aged identity. If our self-appraisal is thorough and honest, we may find flaws—and then set out to correct them.

What hinders this process in some is that as children or adolescents they went through the usual period of flux, wondering what they would be when they grew up, discovering which roles or manners brought the greatest rewards from others, trying to find out who they were. But unlike most, when they arrived at an identity in early adulthood, they saw it as a final goal, a permanent truth, rather than a waystation that would soon have to be left behind.

By middle age, most of us are reasonably aware of our growth as persons, and of our very different requirements and expectations in this phase of life. But reasonable awareness is not enough. We need to make a conscious self-appraisal, a reconsideration of who we are and what we want; only then will we be able to make a series of calculations for the midcourse correction that will put us on the best track for the present and the future.

Such reappraisal is a common part of the middle-aged experience, at least for thoughtful and successful persons. Professor Neugarten, in her study of middle-aged professional and university people, reported, "Middle age is a period of heightened sensitivity to one's position within a complex social environment . . . reassessment of the self is the prevailing theme." Dr. Neugarten also found that in middle age people experienced a satisfying change in self-concept; both married and single persons felt that middle age marked the beginning of a period in which latent talents and capacities could be put to use in new ways.

Using one's self in new ways can be frightening, and in *Gift from the Sea,* Anne Morrow Lindbergh has written eloquently of the fear people feel of changing themselves in mid-life, and of the potential for new joy that lies in mastering the fear:

> Is it not possible that middle age can be looked upon as a period of second flowering, second growth, even a kind of second adolescence? The signs that presage growth, so similar, it seems to me, to those in early adolescence: discontent, restlessness, doubt, despair, longing, are interpreted falsely . . . as signs of approaching death.

Instead of facing them, one runs away.... Anything, rather than
stand still and learn from them. One tries to cure the signs of
growth, to exorcise them, as if they were devils, when really they
might be angels of annunciation.

Angels of annunciation of what? Of a new stage of living when,
having shed many of the physical struggles, the worldly ambitions,
the material encumbrances of active life, one might be free to fulfill
the neglected side of one's self. One might be free for growth of
mind, heart, and talent.

Although earlier chapters have dealt with some of the modifications we make in our time of "second flowering," in this chapter
we have concerned ourselves with making changes consonant with
our new identity in a broad and philosophical way. In fact, some of
the changes are not philosophical at all, but involve matters mundane and practical. Our homes, for example. Many families have
remained in a particular neighborhood because they were reluctant
to uproot the children from schools or friends. Others have maintained a large house or apartment over the years in order to accommodate a large family. Such couples are free, once the children
have left home, to live where they like and in accordance with their
own needs—but some of them fail to make the change because of
inertia, habit, or a feeling of obligation to maintain the old home-
stead for their children's sake. As part of the midcourse correction
they should now ask themselves whether they would prefer to give
up the suburbs for the city, or the city for the country. They can
get rid of the large, expensive, burdensome house and move into a
smaller one or into a modern and easily cared for apartment. This
will save not only time and effort but money, which they can use to
further the new interests of middle age. When the children do come
to visit, they can always be put up on a sofa bed, and if that doesn't
do, treating them to a few nights' lodging at a nearby inn is definitely cheaper than keeping all those empty bedrooms waiting.

A change in residence may be even more radical and entail a
move to another part of the country. Although many people would
enjoy a different climate or life-style, or a different kind of social or
cultural life, few consider such a major move prior to retirement.
The reason, of course, is the need to earn a living. For some, a

change in employment may really be out of the question, but for others, it may be more feasible than they realize. Self-employed professionals, such as doctors, lawyers, or accountants, often buy and sell practices. If a middle-aged professional wants to move from Chicago to Maine, he may find that with his reduced obligations he can easily get along on a reduced income until he has become firmly established in his new community.

For people with jobs, whether blue-collar or white-collar, the situation is often easier, and only rarely harder. A skilled carpenter, laboratory technician, pharmacist, dressmaker, hairdresser, tool-maker, truck driver, teacher, can usually find a job in many sectors of the country. The Departments of Labor of most states and public and private employment agencies can answer questions about the job market in any given locality.

The biggest hindrance to the free movement of employed persons in recent years has been the potential loss of pension benefits. An employee who had spent many years with one company would have a sizable stake in the company pension fund (if it had one), payable at retirement either as a lump sum or in regular installments. Until recently, however, if the employee left before retirement age, he would lose the entire pension. This was patently unfair. But a pension-reform bill enacted by Congress in the summer of 1974 provides for "vesting" employees in such plans after a specified number of years of employment. That is, after a certain number of years of employment, the individual can leave, and whatever equity he has accumulated in the plan remains in his name and becomes payable to him wherever he is, when he reaches the age of eligibility. The employer can choose any one of three options concerning vesting: either the employee gets full vesting after ten years of employment, or 25 per cent vesting after five years but increasing to 100 per cent after fifteen years, or 50 per cent vesting when his age and his years of employment total forty-five but increasing to 100 per cent by 10 per cent for each additional year. While the act covers only those whose employers have pension plans, and omits various groups including federal, state, and local government employees, it does affect an estimated 30 million employees of private firms. For all these people, it is now much more feasible than formerly to move from one company to another and from one part of the country to another. This is particularly important to the middle-aged employee, whose stake in his company pension plan is greatest. With the protection of vesting, the middle-aged employee can now afford to change jobs or locations, if he wants to; he has only his fear of the unknown to overcome.

Bernice comments

Pension plans were not our particular problem, but habit and inertia were. Before Morton and I were married each of us had been living in New York City and summering in East Hampton, 110 miles away, and after we married we continued in the old pattern. Although we had both found the city irresistibly exciting earlier in our lives, we were beginning to feel, like so many other urban people, that the penalties of city life had increased out of all proportion to its rewards. The air had become unbreathable, streets were dangerous and frightening, transportation was agonizingly slow. There seemed always to be a paralyzing strike of some sort, by sanitation workers, subway employees, schoolteachers, or building employees. When our building's elevator operators went on strike, I was sincerely sympathetic to the strikers, but my sympathy didn't help my aching muscles a bit when we had to lug the groceries up eleven very long flights of stairs. And then there were the brownouts, the howling sirens that shattered sleep, the screams for help in the night that woke us up with pounding hearts, the broken water main that flooded the basement and cut off all services for days. It was so hard just to *live.*

And there, in contrast, was peaceful East Hampton, of purest air and unlocked doors. No soot came in the windows, no muggers lurked in the dark, and the only sound to break the stillness of night was the call of a persistent whippoorwill. We planted our garden, fed the birds, watched the osprey dive and the great blue heron stalk, established an eye-to-eye relationship with the pair of seagulls that regarded our waterfront territory as their own. When, in the fall or after winter weekends in the country, we gloomily set out for the city, we could feel our spirits sink lower and lower as we approached the menacing brown miasma that hung over the metropolis. And then, slowly, the idea began to dawn: we didn't really *have* to live in the city at all, so why did we? The children were on their own; both of us were writers and could practice our profession wherever we chose; yet we were supporting two establishments, wasting vast amounts of time and energy running back and forth between them, and spending most of our time in the one we wanted to run away from.

You might think that we made up our minds in five minutes, but we couldn't and didn't. Essentially, we thought of ourselves as city people, intellectually, socially, and financially dependent on urban institutions. And then, East Hampton was in many ways an unknown quantity. We knew *summertime* East Hampton, with its influx of sophisticated vacationers, and we knew winter-weekend East Hampton when we were happy to be alone together to walk on the snowy beach or read in front of a fire. But would it be possible for us to spend a whole winter there? We didn't even know the year-round people; it was conceivable that we might have only each other to talk to for nine long months of the year. And what would we do for plays, movies, concerts, museums, art galleries? True, we never really went to any of those as often as we meant to, but it seemed important to know they were *there*. And what about restaurants? Virtually all the good ones in East Hampton closed up by Thanksgiving at the latest, and after a long hard day's work, I often like to stay out of the kitchen and enjoy a leisurely dinner in a pleasant restaurant. Our uncertainty and misgivings were made worse by the fact that we had one of those huge, high-ceilinged, rent-controlled New York apartments, the kind that everyone envied, and once we gave it up, we could never afford another one like it.

Yet, after long and painful reflection, we finally decided to try it; we would take the leap and, we told each other, if we hated it we could always go back to the city and live in a smaller, less gracious apartment. But if we could deal with full-time country life, we would be saving enough money to visit the city as often as we liked, stay in good hotels, and take in great gulps of culture.

And so we moved. That first winter, we actually did spend a few weekends in city hotels, but soon we began to find it hard to be away from home; there was too much going on. For it turned out that there was a whole colony of people who had remained underground to us while we were *summer people,* but who were all too willing to accept us as full-time residents. (The distinction between *year-round people* and *summer people* is a very important one in our town; it isn't a matter of snobbism, but of community of interests.) We made new friends and acquaintances almost faster than we could keep up with them. Most of them proved to be people like ourselves who had made the move from the city, and who shared many of our interests, tastes, and attitudes. We discovered that there were chamber music concerts from time to time and even some dramatic performances in the winter season that we hadn't known existed. That same year, a small foreign-film theater was opened by four young refugees from the city looking for a way to make a living in our town, and a couple of new restaurants opened under similar auspices.

Today, after three years, we visit the city from time to time for special purposes: to go to some really splendid party, to meet our editors on business, to attend a wedding or funeral, to visit a medical specialist, to be present at some special event (as when my son Eugene accompanied Luciano Pavarotti at Lincoln Center), to see an opera, ballet, or play of particular interest, to go shopping when the list of things we need from Bloomingdale's is running off the page. Since we commonly combine several of these activities in each visit, we make relatively few trips each year. We often stay with our children now instead of in hotels because they have room and we enjoy visiting with them. We also manage to have lunch or dinner with a few old friends each time so that we don't lose contact. While every trip is exhilarating and enriching, we are always happy and somewhat relieved to get back home. Uprooting and transplanting ourselves was a difficult thing to do, but now that we have taken root, we feel it was one of the best things we have done.

Speaking of visiting with old friends brings us to another, often difficult, kind of midcourse correction: the reappraisal of old friendships, and the weeding out of those that are no longer suited to the people we now are.

Each of us has a few old and cherished friends—people we have been close to for many years, people who have shared with us their happiness and ours, their troubles and ours. If we live near them, we probably see them often, but even if we have moved far apart and meet only at long intervals, our friendship remains alive, strong, important. For despite physical distance and long periods without contact, friendships keep their vitality if the friends change and mature in compatible ways. Whenever we meet we can bridge the time gap quickly by bringing each other up to date on personal news and exchanging ideas about books, people, current events, or whatever interests us. We feel as close as we ever did because we are still a "good fit."

In contrast, by middle age most of us have a large number of leftover "friends" from earlier years with whom, if we think about it, we realize we no longer have anything in common. Some of them simply bore us; others actually annoy us by their attitudes or behavior. Some of them hang on to us for their own benefit although they have nothing to offer us in return, some hang on (as bored as we) because they don't know how to let go. They may be old school chums, former Army buddies, ex-next-door neighbors, erstwhile co-workers in some organization, or people who were in the next office on some long-ago job. The community of interest we once shared has long since evaporated and there is nothing left except the habit of seeing each other.

Good old Charlie and Muriel call whenever they're in from Tucson and we feel obliged to welcome them. Even worse are good old Bud and Shirley, who live nearby and often invite us to dinner or parties; fearful of hurting their feelings, we accept a certain percentage of the invitations and then return them, knowing each time that we are letting ourselves in for a long, dull, meaningless evening.

Why ever do we do it? We shouldn't. When acquaintances become obsolete and inappropriate, they should be weeded out just as ruthlessly as the out-of-style clothes that would fill our closets if we let them stay there. It's much easier to cast off clothes than friends, but when we are reviewing and revising so much else in middle age, we should carefully and methodically discard outworn and meaningless relationships in order to make room for new and meaningful ones.

Middle age is, in fact, a particularly good time for making friends; sociological studies show that it is second only to adolescence as a period for forming new relationships. This is a result of the new activities, the new interests, and the new freedom typical of this time of life. When you move, join a new organization, change your job, start a hobby, attend a course, you are bound to meet many new people, and you are likely to find that some of them seem better attuned to you than some of the people you have known for many years. But to take full advantage of these opportunities, you must consciously and deliberately make *room* for the new friendships; like any good gardener, you must prune away the deadwood, pull up the weaker or failing plants, and give the vigorous new ones the best chance to grow and flourish.

Morton comments

I will be deliberately vague in what I have to say here, in order not to hurt someone's feelings. For even now I feel a sense of responsibility and of irrational guilt about an old friend. Ron and I were close friends in our teens; I admired his poise and self-assurance with girls, and he admired my admiration. In young adulthood we remained good friends, though it was clear that our tastes and our interests were far apart. By the time I had reached my 40's, I had nothing in common with Ron except our long history and his tendency to call upon me for help with his increasing personal problems. It took me a long while to realize that for years he had never phoned me or met me for lunch except to tell me about his troubles or to boast of his latest sexual conquests. It was painful for me to admit that his friendship was totally selfish, ungiving, and juvenile, and that he wasn't actually interested in *me* at all. It was difficult for me to tactfully and slowly disengage myself from Ron, feeling guilty all the while because I knew that he would never understand why I was avoiding him. Yet in the end I was freed, and feel that my freedom is right and good. I am writing about this here because I want to offer encouragement and reassurance to those who have a similar problem but hesitate to seek a similar solution.

The new friendships formed in middle age, though more compatible than many old ones, are less homogeneous and therefore particularly enriching and stimulating. Most notably, the middle-aged have a broader age range in their friendships than the very young or the very old. It is common for people from the upper 30's to the lower 60's to mingle easily, and for close friendships to form between people as much as ten or fifteen years apart. To some extent, this is due to the variety of roles the middle-aged person plays, sometimes being sought out as an adviser by younger neighbors and acquaintances, sometimes being the most active and youthful member of a civic organization, and so on. To some extent, too, the broadened age distribution of friendships is the result of the remarriages of the divorced and widowed, a few of whom marry persons a good bit younger or older than themselves (though this is not, statistically, the rule) and, through them, enlarge the circle of friendships.

Interestingly, these days far more than ever before, one's grown children are often a source of friends younger than oneself. As they move into and beyond their late 20's, their relationship with us tends to change into more of a peer relationship than any of us had with our parents. It is not uncommon for contemporary parents to occasionally attend their adult children's parties or invite them to their own; they sometimes go to dinner and to cultural events with each other and each other's friends. And once in a while, as has been the case with us, their friends are halfway between their age and ours, and become our friends as well as theirs.

Talking about the change in the relationship of parents to their grown children brings us to a related aspect of the midcourse correction, the need to adapt to the new roles of mother-in-law and father-in-law. Typically, we first assume these roles in middle age, and with no particular preparation, yet they definitely require a new self-image in some areas so that we can modify our behavior accordingly. Incidentally, though we use the term "in-law," the midcourse correction is actually called for as soon as an adult son or daughter is paired with someone premaritally, for it is at that point that we must begin to recognize their identity and their rights as a couple.

In practice, many people find it difficult to make such a behavior modification adequately; instead, they continue to act like parents to their children, guiding, criticizing, giving unsought advice, seeking to exert control, and subtly—or not so subtly—interfering in the relationship between the two young people. Some years ago, sociologist John L. Thomas made a study of about 7000 Roman Catholic marriages that had ended in divorce and found that problems with in-laws were the most common cause of divorce in the first year of marriage. Blood and Wolfe, in their study of 900 marriages, found that while in-law troubles rated only fifth as an overall cause of strife throughout marriage, the great bulk of such problems occurred during the early years of the marriage, and some began during the honeymoon.

Even though today young people are somewhat less concerned about parental approval than when these studies were conducted, the situation is still basically the same. The problem is really two-fold, for it is not only that some parents can't seem to relinquish the power and authority they used to have when their children were younger, but also that some children, even though adult and married, have trouble giving up their emotional and/or financial dependence on Mom and Dad. If it is the child who clings to the old relationship, it is up to the parent to make the correction anyway and gently but firmly push the dependent youngster out of the nest.

The innumerable old mother-in-law jokes were based on a solid core of truth: many studies have shown that mothers-in-law are far more often a source of difficulty for the young couple than fathers-in-law, although fathers-in-law, too, are capable of making trouble. The problem is most often due to a carryover of formerly suitable, but now highly *un*suitable, parental helpfulness; however well meant, it is now demeaning, intrusive, and disruptive. A case in point:

Sally E. had been a devoted, efficient, and admirable mother to her children; indeed, she had no interest in life which even compared with mothering. When her son Elliot became engaged to Anne, whom he had known for several years, Sally was delighted. She had always wanted a daughter, and she treated Anne with great affection and repeated offers of assistance of every kind. She managed to become just a bit of a nuisance with her overflowing helpfulness about the details of the wedding, but all went well and Anne and Elliot were married in an aura of good feeling all around.

Right after the honeymoon, the young couple moved to a distant city to which Elliot had been reassigned by the firm he worked for. Anne, a nurse, found a job there almost immediately, and what with working full-time, shopping for furniture, having the apartment painted, and making new friends, almost everything the pair owned was still in cartons two weeks later. It was just at this point that Elliot's mother phoned and said she couldn't *wait* to see them in their new apartment. Elliot, who had answered the phone, gently explained that they weren't ready for a guest yet, but Sally said nonsense! she wasn't a *guest*, she was *Mother*, and besides, if they were both so busy, she could do a lot to help get things in order. Elliot, unaccustomed to overruling his mother, weakly said all right. When he told Anne the news she wasn't happy about it, but she said little since she didn't want to quarrel with Elliot or offend Sally, of whom she was really quite fond.

Sally arrived on Thursday evening, looked appraisingly at the apartment, and made some approving remarks as well as a few suggestions. The three went out to a restaurant for dinner since, as Anne explained, they hadn't had time to do anything about the kitchen yet. In the morning, as Anne and Elliot were getting ready to leave for work, they started to tell Sally about the points of interest in the city, but she brushed their suggestions aside; they mustn't bother their heads about her, she said, she really preferred to be on her own.

That evening, Elliot arrived home first and found that Sally had a grand surprise waiting: she had worked all day at setting up the kitchen. The dishes were unpacked, washed, and stored away, the pots and pans were all arranged on the pegboard, the cupboards were stocked with staples, canned goods, and spices. Sally had even, incredibly, made her way to a nearby store, bought some ready-made curtains with spring-loaded rods, and had snapped them into place over the kitchen windows. She was exhausted but very proud of her accomplishments. Elliot thanked her profusely, but somewhere in the pit of his stomach he had an uneasy feeling to which he couldn't give a name.

When Anne arrived and was shown the wonders Mother Sally had achieved, she was wide-eyed with astonishment, but curiously silent. She thanked Sally tersely and then had almost nothing to say for the rest of the evening. Elliot had not expected her to be wild with enthusiasm, but he *did* think she might have shown more gratitude for what, after all, had been a well-meant gesture and a good deal of hard work. Sally, for her part, was disappointed and disillusioned; she figured that she hadn't really sized up Anne cor-

rectly after all, and that she was far from the loving and apprecia-
tive daughter-in-law she had seemed to be back home.

They got through the next day, Saturday, peacefully enough by
going to a museum and a movie, and on Sunday, Sally flew home.
The moment she boarded the plane, Elliot and Anne began the first
big fight of their marriage. By the time they got back to the apartment, Anne was crying and almost hysterical with anger, while
Elliot alternated between trying to calm her down and to defend
his mother. Finally, Anne ripped the new curtains from the windows and threw them into the trash. When Elliot became enraged
by her act she proceeded wildly to empty every cupboard in the
kitchen, haphazardly piling dishes and groceries on the counter, the
table, the chairs, the floor. By the time she was done, she and Elliot
were screaming at each other, and Anne was ready to pack a bag
and go home to *her* mother.

Fortunately, she was too exhausted to do anything at that
juncture, and after a good night's sleep (with the help of a pill) the
whole quarrel seemed a bit overblown. Elliot wisely suggested that
they both take the day off from work, go shopping for new curtains,
and do the whole job over again, together, the way they had
planned to do it in the first place. Long before evening, the crisis
had passed, but the emotional debris of that quarrel took weeks to
clean up. There were many long, and sometimes acerbic, discussions before Elliot could admit that he had been too obedient and
dutiful a son for too long, and that in this case he should have
supported his wife's position and not his mother's. He finally perceived that his mother failed to recognize him and Anne as adults,
ignoring their right to decide when to invite her to visit, and even
depriving them of the right to fix up their own first home. Anne, for
her part, grudgingly admitted that she, too, had been at fault: she
had not had the courage to make it plain to Elliot that his mother's
visit was untimely and should be canceled, or to tell Sally clearly
and honestly that she had meddled and usurped Anne's place. But
one cannot blame Anne for that lapse because she was far too young
and inexperienced to face her mother-in-law as one adult woman to
another. By the time she is 40, both she and Sally will have no
trouble understanding whose kitchen it is and who is in charge.

For the present, Sally is completely in the dark. The young

couple has not told her the truth, but has managed, for nearly a year, to sidestep further visits. Sally doesn't know that she has to make a midcourse correction and she persists, through letters and telephone calls, in trying to be motherly and helpful. When her suggestions and questions about every aspect of the couple's life are ignored, she is puzzled and hurt. Unfortunately, she is likely to remain so unless she finds out that in-laws should be loving, supportive, and friendly, but helpful *only when asked*. In short, they should mind their own business.

Making the midcourse transition to appropriate in-law behavior requires, first, awareness, and second, deliberate and persistent effort, for modifying one's habitual behavior can be very difficult. These days it can be particularly so for parents, since so many young people have views of sex and marriage that are far more flexible and innovative than those of their elders. We're referring primarily to the shift toward premarital relationships—not just sexual relationships, but the new folkway of openly living together, unwed. A generation or two ago, it was still known as "living in sin," but today, few young people see any sin in it. Fortunately, a good many parents share their views, but many others do not. They either openly and strenuously disapprove, or pretend not to know and avoid all social contact with the young couple except in neutral surroundings. Even some of the parents who are all in favor of a trial marriage rather than a real one and a hasty divorce may remain uneasy and uncomfortable about the situation when they are dealing with their own peer group. Part of their discomfort is often based on the fact that our language has not yet provided us with a proper label by which to designate a son's or daughter's nonlegal mate, one which allows us to signify our respect for the relationship. When the relationship is a serious and stable one, our own suggestion is that we use the terms "son-out-of-law" and "daughter-out-of-law." They sound a bit jocular, but they are a candid statement to the world, and to the young people themselves, that the parents recognize the relationship as important, respected, and a valid alternative to legal marriage. Whether or not these particular labels achieve wide usage, some new terminology will have to come along to fill the gap, and when it does, the existence of suitable words will help parents make the transition to feeling comfortable within themselves.

Still greater difficulties in transition are experienced by parents whose children enter into alliances even less conventional by the parents' standards. Interracial pairings are one example: even among people who have never had any conscious feelings of prejudice, there is often acute discomfort in trying to act the parts of in-laws to a person whose entire life experience has been so different from their own.

Even more difficult for many is the task of adopting something like an appropriate in-law role when one's son or daughter has entered into a homosexual alliance. Until recently, homosexual couples usually pretended to be just roommates, and parents—even when they suspected the truth—went along with the pretense to spare themselves the burden of openly adjusting to the reality. Today, with so many homosexuals having come out in the open, particularly those living in stable relationships, parents are more often forced to acknowledge the couple as a couple and to make whatever corrections are required in order to adapt.

The mate of one's child, whether unwed, Jewish, black, Oriental, or gay, isn't going to disappear just because the parents object or disapprove; they will either have to find a way to relate to the newcomer and take the partnership in stride or lose all, or almost all, contact with the son or daughter. Those who simply cannot deal with the situation effectively may find it helpful to read widely on the subject, discuss the matter with trusted friends (who will undoubtedly be less emotional and more realistic about it), or, if necessary, seek counseling from a qualified therapist.

Once you have gotten over all the hurdles of becoming an in-law, you may have yet another new role awaiting you, the much-vaunted (and deservedly so) one of grandparent. But here again, a set of adjustments is called for, for when one becomes a grandparent, the temptation to butt in is almost irresistible.

First of all, remember that the new baby isn't *your* child; you had your chance at child-rearing, and now it's someone else's. Anyway, styles in child-rearing change from one generation to the

next and there is little evidence to prove that one style is significantly better than another. So while it is quite possible for you to
feel that three-year-old Suzy should have been toilet-trained long
ago, that her table manners are barbaric, and that dirty blue jeans
are hardly proper dress for a little girl, it is also possible that your
son and daughter feel just the opposite, and that they are just as
likely to be right. None of your beliefs will in any way change Suzy's
upbringing; what they *will* change, if you aren't careful, is your
relationship with Suzy's parents. To put it plainly, both as in-laws
and as grandparents you have to keep your adverse opinions to
yourself (no, not even communicating them by disapproving silence) unless they are expressly requested. Even then, you would do
well to play the role of adviser in an adult-to-adult fashion: offer
suggestions, but don't issue edicts or pronunciamentos.

Despite the occasional self-control and self-modification
required by grandparenthood, it is unquestionably one of the great
plusses of middle age. There is enormous luxury in being able to
play with and listen to and cuddle and delight in a loved and loving
little child—and then go home to peace and quiet, while the parents
take care of the little dear when it's become sleepy and cross. And
it's even a treat, and an enriching and renewing experience, to have
grandchildren all to yourself for a whole day, a weekend, or perhaps
a long vacation. For while a lengthy stint may tire the out-of-prac-
tice grandparent, it is a temporary thing, with an ending in sight,
and nothing at all like the unrelenting task of being a full-time
parent. Perhaps it is precisely that that makes grandparenthood so
marvelous.

Just when you have dealt with the fact that your own children
are all grown up and full-fledged people, and you have tasted the
first delights of being a grandparent, it is highly likely that you will
have to face the fact that there are beginning to be some changes in
your parents. As they grow older, and you begin to feel responsible
for them, you are forced to make yet another midcourse correction;
you now perceive yourself, for the first time, not as having parents
to turn to and lean upon but rather as having parents who now turn
to lean upon you. As Dr. Roger L. Gould, assistant professor of

psychiatry at UCLA's School of Medicine, wrote in the *American Journal of Psychiatry:*

> There is a difference between living in the world with live, healthy, and powerful parents in the background ready to support you, and living with enfeebled, dependent parents in the background. If anything, the changes that take place in one's parents and in one's children would suggest that . . . necessity for change is as imperative as in the period before age 21.

In the next chapter we will talk about the practical problems of dealing with parents who have become so elderly and ailing that they can no longer take care of themselves—the point at which we, in effect, become parents to our parents. Here, however, we want to point out that the psychological problems involved in this transition can be minimized by anticipation. Parents *do* grow old and, in the natural order of things, die before their children do. Their death is bound to be a crisis—but like all crises, it is less severe for those who have not been afraid to look at it ahead of time and begin to adjust to it in imagination.

Moreover, the problems arising from the changes in the parent-child relationship actually have some beneficial effects on the spouse relationship, according to Dr. Gould. During our late 30's and early 40's, as our parents begin to age and turn more toward us, there is some renewal of the old parent-child conflict—only now we, the children, cannot openly express criticism of our older parents because it would make us feel too guilty. We become aware of the finiteness of time, and this time pressure and conflict lead us to turn to the spouse, who is often in a similar position.

Then, during our late 40's and through the 50's, as our parents become feebler and more clearly mortal, we increasingly seek affection and sympathy from our spouses. In this midcourse correction, the spouse, in Dr. Gould's words, "is seen now as a valuable source of companionship in life and less like a parent or source of supplies. Criticisms of the previous years are realigned to take into account this central change." And so we see that even the need to adapt ourselves to the aging and death of our parents is one more source of the increased marital satisfaction which, as we reported earlier, is so characteristic of middle age.

But while it is characteristic, it is not universal. For, as we have already observed, with the departure of the children it becomes painfully clear to some men and women that their marriages have become outworn, meaningless, and unrewarding. Then the midcourse correction required to salvage the potentialities of a rich and joyous middle age is the drastic and painful one of divorce, and the subsequent search for another and more rewarding love relationship. We will discuss this complex subject more fully in Chapter 8.

Finally, the ultimate component of the midcourse correction involves perceiving oneself, too, as mortal, and as destined for old age. It is not a paradox that we have been speaking about the ample time and the rich possibilities of middle age, and yet raise the issue of what comes after it; middle age is the proper time to think ahead and to make sure our long-range plans are in good order. Many of us have emotional reasons for pushing aside thoughts of retirement so we say that it is too far off to think about now, or that it will be predetermined by our employers and there isn't anything we can do about it anyway. Sociologist John A. Clausen points out that most men (and presumably women) are somewhat ambivalent about retirement, even those who have been very successful. For most, he finds, it means a lowered standard of living, and a loss of valued social contacts; for some, it is the end of their central purpose in life, a loss of power and prestige. For those who have been failures, it destroys any lingering hope or fantasy of a late-blooming success.

But whatever one's reasons for not wanting to face it, it is a mistake to let retirement plans wait for the future, for according to a recent survey, half of those who are currently retired say they retired unexpectedly. Therefore, whether you plan to retire at all, or have selected some given age for it, by the time you are in your 40's you should begin to think about a retirement program as a bulwark against the fifty-fifty chance that you will need one before you expect to.

We won't bother to talk about the obvious aspects of retirement planning, the array of pension plans, annuities, and Keogh Plans, the shifting of funds from stocks to real estate or vice versa, or from either or both to safe, interest-yielding investments. These are matters to discuss with your lawyer, accountant, insurance broker, or investment counselor, or possibly all four.

A less complicated step in planning for your future, but one which may be emotionally difficult, is to stop doling out money to your children if they are old enough to support themselves. It is fine to send them to college, but you don't have to support them until they become certified brain surgeons and you don't have to buy them a house in the suburbs. Such continued support is a way of keeping your children dependent on you when they shouldn't be, and it is also a way of leaving yourself in straitened circumstances later in life. You probably had some financial struggles when you were young and it won't hurt your children to have some, too. The Roman emperors kept their people pacified with endless handouts, and destroyed the traditional hard-working Roman character. You don't want to do that to your children—and unless you're as rich as a Roman emperor, you don't really want any extra financial obligations at this time of your life. This doesn't mean that you should stop giving presents at the usual times, or fail to help out in a crisis. It does mean that you should begin to think about the importance of extra money in the bank after you have retired.

For you mustn't delude yourself that to support grown children is to cast bread upon the waters. The bread is most likely to sink and never be seen again. Matilda White Riley and Harris Schrank report, in *Aging and Society,* that while grown children and grandchildren give emotional support and companionship to aging parents, they do not support them financially. Public-opinion polls show that the majority of Americans believe that it is every person's responsibility to save for his older years if he wants to supplement his income from Social Security and retirement funds. So once you have reared your children, let them take care of themselves, and plan to take care of *your*self in the future. This is not only a realistic plan but one that will best preserve the parent-child relationship in your later years.

Closely related to the above caveat is one more: don't have

relatives come to live with you. It's one thing for a couple of widowed cousins to throw their lot together, but quite another thing for the middle-aged couple to "take in" any widowed, divorced, or never-married relative out of kindness. For one thing, it is usually a financial drain since one can't ever assess Aunt Nellie for all the hidden costs of adding another member to the household. It also robs the couple, at this potentially most intimate and companionable time in their relationship, of the privacy that is essential to such a relationship. Beyond that, it hopelessly complicates whatever long-range retirement plans the couple might want to make, limiting their freedom of choice as to the size and location of their home, their choice of activities, and even their freedom to travel.

Speaking of choice of activities, a significant part of planning for retirement is the advance preparation for the use of one's leisure. We have already dealt with this subject but it is worth repeating here that those who are most successful in their retirement are those who, well ahead of time, laid and perfected plans to make it a busy and important time and not an interlude between life and death. Drs. Riley and Schrank find that positive acceptance of retirement is greatest among those who maintain their prior levels of activity; clearly, this can best be done by those with activities which can be expanded enough to substitute for their relinquished work. Given adequate health and income, such people are not likely to experience retirement as a time of loss, of withering, of waiting to die, but rather as a new stage of continued active existence, with its own special goals and rewards.

Lastly, the most mature and realistic of all acts comprising the midcourse correction is the candid admission that you yourself will one day die, and so must have a will. It is apparently hard for us to face the fact of mortality, for only about one out of every four adult Americans has executed a will. In part, this may be due to ignorance, since many people assume that if they die, the entire estate will automatically go to the spouse. This is true in some states, but not in most. Generally, some portion automatically goes to the children and the spouse can be left with as little as one third. In the absence of children, it is often the right of other close relatives to claim a share of the inheritance. You can save a great deal of confusion and hard feelings if you make certain that your estate goes where you want it to. Although most people want, ultimately, to leave something to their children, it seems unreasonable for them to share in the estate while they are young and energetic and the surviving spouse is not. With the kind of trust that exists within truly companionable couples, it is often agreed that the surviving spouse will inherit the entire estate and will then rewrite his or her will to make whatever provisions for the children that the pair had earlier agreed upon.

In any case, even if your state does make the spouse the sole inheritor in the absence of a will, it can take the survivor an incredibly long time, struggling through endless red tape all the way, to settle the estate and take title to the assets. It is an ultimate kindness to avoid this unnecessary hardship, and it can be done in a matter of minutes and for as little as $25 or $50 in most places. This, of course, would be for the simplest kind of will, but if you have none at all, you can call your lawyer and ask for an "emergency" will; at your leisure, you can consider the matter in more detail and draw up a more complex (and more expensive) document if you need or want to.

And now, if you have really opened your mind to all of the foregoing possibilities, there is a good chance that you will make some or most of the corrections to your trajectory through life, and will be right on course for Prime Time.

7 *The Reality Factor*

DEALING WITH THE ILLS THAT
MIDDLE-AGED FLESH IS HEIR TO

Although the focus of this book is on the new potential for making contemporary middle age the Prime Time of life, it would be less than honest to ignore the fact that mid-life presents a number of special problems. Every stage of life has its own unique problems; those of middle age are often particularly disturbing because we tend to view them as signs of the end of well-being and of a decline toward death. Highest on the list of mid-life vexations, indeed, are those diseases which most often begin to cause trouble at this time. Fortunately, to be forewarned is to be forearmed. What follows is a brief look at the major middle-age health problems and the latest information about how to deal with them; you don't have to just sit there and worry—you can really do something.

Ask virtually any middle-aged person what health problem looms as the greatest threat to life, and he or she is almost certain to give the right answer: heart disease. Throughout the population (all ages combined), deaths from diseases of the heart outnumber those from cancer, the second major cause of death, by more than two to one. For men, the risk is particularly high; in fact, the average healthy American male has a one-in-five chance of having a heart attack before he is 65, and about a one-in-fifteen chance of dying from it. By middle age, coronary artery disease—the cause of nearly all heart attacks—is a major killer, accounting for roughly one third of all deaths of men between 45 and 54.

But don't despair. While we have no defense against cancer

except to avoid known or suspected carcinogens such as tobacco, and to have frequent and thorough medical checkups, we can do a good deal to prevent or minimize the development of coronary artery disease and therefore to reduce the risk of heart attack.

In order to do so, we first have to understand what causes that disease and its serious consequences. Some of the causes are, unfortunately, *not* within our control. For instance, our sex. You will surely have noticed that in any discussion of heart attack, the emphasis is on its occurrence in males—and for good reason: coronary artery disease is only about one third as common a cause of death in women as it is in men. Women seem to have a built-in protection against coronary artery disease; by early middle age, however, this begins to fail them, for at that time of life the incidence of coronary artery disease in women starts to rise and continues to do so steadily until, by late life, the rates for men and women are equal. Yet even when women do suffer from coronary artery disease, its symptoms tend to have a much slower onset, and sudden deaths from heart attack tend to be far less common in women than in men.

Because women's superior resistance to coronary artery disease begins to wane at about the time of menopause, it has long been believed—and still is, by many doctors—that ovarian function is the protective mechanism, and that it is the cessation of ovarian function, bringing about the climacteric, that accounts for the rise in women's susceptibility to this dread disease. But there are good reasons for considering ovarian function only a part—and perhaps a minor part—of the picture.

For one thing, the advantage that women have over men in their earlier years exists only for white women; for another, it is far smaller for those women with a low standard of living than those with a high one; for a third, even affluent white women have no advantage over men if they suffer from diabetes or hypertension (high blood pressure). Clearly, many things other than the presence or absence of estrogen in the body influence the development of coronary artery disease. In fact, trials of supposedly prophylactic doses of estrogen administered to postmenopausal women and to men who had survived one heart attack or were suffering from some other disease have produced only variable (and hence inconclusive) results—and, incidentally, have increased the incidence of stroke in these patients.

Reviewing this whole question in *Menopause and Aging,* a recent publication of the Department of Health, Education, and Welfare, Dr. Robert H. Furman, professor of medicine at the University of Indiana, concludes that menopause is not the major factor in women's loss of resistance to coronary artery disease, and that if ovarian function does provide partial protection prior to menopause, it is some aspect of that function that has not yet been spelled out. These conclusions remain highly controversial.

In any case, the absence of ovarian function is only one of a number of factors that predispose the individual to the development of coronary artery disease. Among other factors that do so are an inherited predisposition to the disease (as indicated by a family history of heart attacks), obesity, smoking, failure to take regular exercise, diabetes, high blood pressure, high serum cholesterol, and, perhaps, stress. You can't do anything about your sex or about your family history, but you can do a lot about the rest of the factors. All of them are important, but possibly the most important of all is the very one you can almost always easily control quite simply—by diet—namely, serum (blood) cholesterol. (There are, to be sure, a very few individuals whose cholesterol is virtually uncontrollable, but such cases are extremely rare.)

Everyone has heard about cholesterol by now, but not everyone understands just what it is, how it does its damage, and how easy it is to deal with. Cholesterol is a complex organic substance that is a constituent of all animal fats and oils, and is present in many body tissues and in the blood. The body actually synthesizes a certain amount of cholesterol, since it is needed in various metabolic processes. The trouble comes about when we oversupply our bodies with cholesterol by means of the foods we eat; this excess supply, unneeded by the tissues, circulates in the blood as serum cholesterol, but the problem is that it doesn't continue to circulate. Cholesterol tends to precipitate out, stick to the blood-vessel walls, and stay there.

That's what makes it a crucial element in the genesis of heart attacks. For virtually all heart attacks begin not in the heart muscle itself, but rather in the coronary arteries that supply the muscle with nourishing blood so it can do its work. While heart attacks in middle age seem to occur suddenly, in the great majority of cases they have been preceded by many years of developing coronary artery disease due to the gradual buildup of the excess cholesterol on the arterial walls. The process may start as early as infancy, but in any case it begins many years before the heart attack. During those years, the circulating mushy, yellow, fatty cholesterol accumulates on the arterial walls, where it is held in waxy globs known as *plaques*. When they become large enough or numerous enough, they seriously impede the flow of blood; the arteries become like pipes so corroded by rust that water can scarcely pass through them. The accumulation of plaques in the blood vessels is *atheroma;* the disease of the arteries atheroma causes is *atherosclerosis* (a type of hardening of the arteries); and atherosclerosis of those special arteries that nourish the heart muscle itself is *coronary artery disease.*

When coronary artery disease becomes far enough advanced, it cuts off the flow of blood to some part of the heart muscle; it does so either by restricting the flow to a trickle or by creating blood clots (due to impeded flow) which break loose and lodge in a small branch coronary artery, blocking it completely. When either thing happens, the affected part of the heart ceases to function and the victim suffers a heart attack. If the affected area of the heart muscle is small, it dies and is replaced by scar tissue (an *infarct*), leaving the heart impaired but its owner alive; if the affected area is large, the heart—and its owner—die.

The cholesterol buildup that is responsible for this owes something, it is generally thought, to the interplay of the many factors we named above—but the major factor is excessive cholesterol intake, without which the others could hardly cause atherosclerosis. Why do we take in excess cholesterol? Because our American diet includes a great deal of meat, butter, whole milk, cream, eggs, and rich baked goods and desserts. Organ meats such as brains and sweetbreads—favorites of gourmets—are extraordinarily high in cholesterol. So are creamy cheeses. Many of those good things your mother stuffed you with, hoping to make you robust and healthy, are full of cholesterol. A diet high in such foods slowly and inexorably damages the coronary arteries and predisposes the individual to heart attack. Many doctors now believe that even children should not eat unlimited amounts of high-cholesterol foods; as for middle-aged people, they most definitely should avoid them altogether. If it takes the word of an expert to convince you that a high serum cholesterol level precedes coronary artery disease, and that lowering the level can prevent the disease, listen to what the world-renowned cardiothoracic surgeon, Dr. Christiaan Barnard, has to say:

> From the epidemiologists, then, we have learned two things: (1) people who eat a diet high in animal fat have a higher incidence of coronary disease than those who do not; (2) people with a high blood cholesterol level are more likely to develop symptoms due to atheroma than those whose blood cholesterol levels are low. Now it can easily be shown by direct and rigorously controlled experiments that, keeping all other circumstances the same, the blood cholesterol concentration of volunteers can be manipulated at will by feeding them food containing different amounts of animal fats.

Are you supposed to go hungry? Certainly not. The modifications needed to change your diet to one that is low in cholesterol are really not at all dramatic or hard to endure. You can easily stick to your diet when dining with friends or in a restaurant and you can always get enough to eat. Unless you have had more drastic advice from your doctor, the following guidelines should be adequate to lower your serum cholesterol markedly.

Eat only lean meat. Trim off all the fat you can see (yes, even the crispy part on the roast beef), and give up altogether meats that are heavily marbled with fat and hence untrimmable.

Limit your meat meals to a few a week; substitute poultry and fish (but not shellfish, which is high in cholesterol) the rest of the time.

Switch from butter to a soft (unhydrogenated) margarine. The all-safflower kind is especially good.

Use vegetable oils such as safflower, corn, or soy for cooking and for salad dressing. Walnut oil, which you may not be familiar with since it is sold only in natural-food stores or departments, is particularly delicious on salads. All of these oils are partly polyunsaturated and actually tend to reduce serum cholesterol levels. Monosaturates, such as olive oil, do not add cholesterol but they don't take any away, either. If you are particularly fond of the flavor of olive oil, mix it with your polyunsaturated oil.

Avoid all rich cheese (there are many excellent skim-milk cheeses on the market). Avoid cream (either sweet or sour), whole milk (use skim), ice cream (ice milk is lower in cholesterol, fruit ice has none).

Avoid rich desserts, chocolate, cocoanut, and egg yolks.

Eggs have been in the news a great deal of late because in the last year or two, as the public has become increasingly cholesterol-conscious and begun to shun eggs, the industry has felt the pinch and engaged in a barrage of advertising to try to boost sales of its product. Such advertising has elicited heated protest from many scientists. One of them, Professor William E. Connor, a cholesterol expert in the Department of Internal Medicine of the College of Medicine, University of Iowa, has stated: "Egg yolk is the highest source of cholesterol in the human diet." In his experiments, Dr. Connor found that when healthy people ate a cholesterol-free diet to which two to four eggs a day had been added, their blood cholesterol levels ran 10 to 50 per cent higher than when they ate an otherwise comparable cholesterol-free diet without eggs. In the same series of experiments, when monkeys were fed several eggs a day, their cholesterol levels tripled in a month, and after a year their arteries were clogged with atherosclerotic plaques. A matched group of other monkeys on a regular diet developed no such atherosclerosis.

Dr. Connor also pointed out that in those parts of the world where heart disease is virtually unknown, the average blood cholesterol level is 140 to 180 milligrams per cubic centimeter. "When you get above 220, you're in the high-risk group for heart disease," Dr. Connor said. Some doctors think even 220 is too high, but most middle-aged Americans are at that level or even higher.

There are a number of excellent low-cholesterol cookbooks on the market; a few of them are listed in the bibliography, and owning and using a couple of them will make your switch to a low-cholesterol diet virtually painless.

We won't go into the details of the other factors implicated in coronary artery disease, or the degree to which controlling those factors can reduce the risk of death, but each of them is now thought to play a measurable part in the overall outcome. A remarkable decline in the coronary death rate in recent years is the result of growing public awareness of the danger of high cholesterol levels, smoking, and overweight, and the value of regular exercise and the control of blood pressure. Major advances in medical research and the care of heart patients have also been partly responsible for the change. Between 1940 and 1963 there had been an 18 per cent increase in the national death rate due to heart disease, but between 1963 and 1974, there was a decline of between 10 and 11 per cent. Dr. Peter Frommer of the National Heart and Lung Institute made the announcement in 1974 and said, "We're very much impressed by this. These changes seem to be real, not a figment of the statistics."

At about the same time, confirmation came from Dr. Hollis S. Ingraham, New York State Health Commissioner, who reported that the results of a statewide survey showed that among New York residents, between 1963 and 1970, "The heart disease mortality rate for male residents showed a 10.5 per cent decrease while the same rate for females dropped 7.2 per cent."

A large-scale and dramatic study of the effects of cholesterol and smoking on the rate of heart disease began in 1973 in North Karelia, Finland, where the Finnish government and the World Health Organization are conducting a five-year experiment to determine why the 186,000 residents of that region have the world's highest incidence of heart attack, and whether it can be substantially lowered by changes in diet and tobacco use.

What makes this project of special interest is that the North Karelian men get plenty of exercise—they are largely lumberjacks—and they are not subject to the kind of stress usually associated with urban living. Yet every year, 9.3 per thousand of them between the ages of 20 and 64 are stricken by heart attacks; a single community in the region, Ilomantsi, has the highest rate of all, 14.9 per thousand. By comparison, nearby Helsinki has a rate of only 5.3 per thousand and Sofia, Bulgaria, about 1 per thousand, believed to be the world's lowest rate.

The North Karelian diet is highly suspect as the cause of the trouble. Formerly, this area was so poor that its inhabitants sold all of their butter and cream and drank only skim milk, but in recent times the income level has improved somewhat and the North Karelians no longer sell their cream but use it themselves. They favor a cuisine that is almost devoid of vegetables but extraordinarily high in butterfat. They eat quantities of buttery pastries and like their herring served with lumps of fat.

In the current experiment, Finnish health officials, the local newspapers and radio stations, and union leaders and teachers are all collaborating in an educational campaign to get the North Karelians to eat more vegetables, to use less butter and other animal fat, and to drink skim milk rather than the creamy product they are accustomed to. (The campaign is also directed against smoking, but the major emphasis of the researchers is on dietary change.) Tens of thousands of North Karelians have already begun to change their eating habits as a result of the campaign. The study will run until 1978, by which time it is expected that the results will definitely show the extent to which a high-cholesterol diet is responsible for a high rate of heart attack in a given population, and the extent to which dietary change can reduce that rate. Doctors in America and all over the world are eagerly awaiting the answers.

In the meantime, you can perform your own experiment by asking your doctor to check your serum cholesterol, and then have him do so again after you have been on a low-cholesterol diet for a year or so.

Morton comments

Which is what I myself did, with remarkable results. Two years ago, as part of my annual medical checkup, my doctor ordered a serum cholesterol test. The result came back 260 milligrams. That's well into the danger area, but I wasn't worried because I was uninformed. That is, ignorant. But Bernice wasn't ignorant, and she *was* worried; she'd been doing a lot of reading about middle-aged medical problems and had become convinced of the importance of taking preventive measures against circulatory and heart disorders. She began a campaign of education and persuasion, and though I wasn't always tractable, I did read the things she asked me to read, and I did see the light. Out went butter and in went margarine; out went cream and in went yogurt; out went meat (most nights of the week) and in went poultry and seafood; and so on. A year and a half later I had another serum cholesterol test and this time the reading was 197—well within the "safe" area. (I put "safe" in quotes because, while low cholesterol readings greatly reduce the risk of heart attack, they do not absolutely guarantee immunity from it.) I was as pleased and proud as if I had done it all myself, and I have been sticking to the rules—without feeling deprived—ever since.

Cholesterol-watching may even have advantages beyond the prevention of heart disease. Dr. Ernst L. Wynder, president of the American Health Foundation in New York City, addressing a seminar of science writers held by the American Cancer Society in March 1974, presented impressive evidence to show that there is a link between a high-fat diet and a high incidence of colon-rectal cancer.

A third advantage to a low-cholesterol diet is that it tends to be a moderate-calorie diet, and thus helpful in weight control. Extra weight is a burden to the heart: if you put on an additional twenty pounds, that's twenty pounds of tissue that your heart has to supply with oxygen and nutrients and from which it has to remove waste products. You also have to carry that twenty pounds around every time you move, and that's hard work. This is one reason that fat people run far greater risks of heart disease than thin ones.

If you are overweight, therefore, you should diet—but carefully. Fad diets are usually poor; not only does the quickly lost weight come back just as quickly as it left, but many "gimmick" diets —especially those that emphasize unlimited fat intake—are positively dangerous. A crash diet that involves partial or total fasting can seriously weaken the individual and do damage to various organs and tissues. The best way to diet is just to eat a little less of everything. In middle age, our metabolic rate begins to slow down, and we don't require as many calories as we used to; it is the tendency to eat as much as we used to, not necessarily more, that makes many people gain weight as they grow older. In addition to cutting down just a little on portion sizes, if you have a special vice—candy, cookies, Danish pastry between meals—try to overcome it; if you can't, at least cut the portions in half. In this case, half a loaf is worse than none but better than a whole one.

While health is more important than any other reason for losing weight, there are a number of others: the pure pleasure of feeling sleek and lithe instead of fat and lumpy is a valid one. So are looking good in clothes (or without them), or being able to scramble around a tennis court with agility or run for a bus with ease. You have probably thought of these advantages yourself, but one you may not have had any inkling of is that fat people don't earn as much money as thin ones. As reported recently in *The New York Times,* Robert Half, the president of a chain of employment agencies bearing his name, conducted a survey involving 15,000 of the agencies' executive clients. He discovered that of 1500 executives who earned between $25,000 and $45,000 a year, only 9 per cent were more than ten pounds overweight, while of 13,500 executives who earned between $10,000 and $20,000, almost 40 per cent were more than 10 *per cent*—a good bit more than ten pounds—overweight. Mr. Half commented that his offices received thousands of requests for thin people but the only request they had ever had for a fat one came from a company that made clothing for overweight men.

Whether or not you choose to consider the financial penalty of overweight a weighty matter or not, there is another that you must take seriously because it is a matter of life and death, and that is the relation of overweight to diabetes mellitus. You don't have to be overweight to become diabetic, but it is often a precipitating factor, as you will see in a moment.

Everyone over 40 should be informed about diabetes because it is very much a disease of middle age. It is ten times as prevalent in people over 45 as in those under that age, and 50 per cent of the presently known 3 million diabetics in the United States were between the ages of 45 and 64 when the diagnosis was made.

People who get diabetes in mid-life are called *maturity-onset* diabetics, as opposed to *juvenile-onset* diabetics, who have had the disease since childhood. Childhood diabetics account for about 30 per cent of all cases of the disease and they suffer from a much more serious form of it than those who get it in middle age. While some maturity-onset diabetics are of normal weight, Dr. Henry Dolger, chief of the Diabetes Clinic at New York's Mt. Sinai Hospital says, "Plain overeating is today accepted as the most common precipitating factor in diabetes. This is not to imply that every overweight person—or even the majority of them—will become diabetic. But at least three of every four adults who became diabetic were overweight before they developed the disease."

The reason that diabetes often develops in overweight persons is that the disease occurs when the body does not produce enough insulin to metabolize the amount of carbohydrate ingested; or, to say exactly the same thing another way, diabetes occurs when a person ingests more carbohydrate than his body's insulin supply can metabolize. For such people, a reduction of carbohydrate intake may be all that is required to restore the body's balance and keep the diabetes under control.

But there are many factors other than diet involved in diabetes onset, too. Heredity plays a large role, and if any of your close relatives have or had the disease, you should report this fact to your doctor and be sure to get frequent checkups. This is particularly important if you are overweight, for the combination of obesity and a family history of diabetes makes one a highly likely candidate. It is still more important if you are a woman, for women are more susceptible to the disease than men, and by middle age they are twice as susceptible. Motherhood apparently plays a role since those women who have borne many children fall prey to the disease more often than those who have not. Mothers of large infants are especially prone to develop it; a woman who has given birth to a child weighing ten pounds or more has a greater than 75 per cent chance of contracting diabetes in middle age. Endocrinologists think that since pituitary growth hormone affects the size of the child, a malfunction in the production of the hormone may have something to do with the disease itself.

The onset of diabetes is insidious and often goes unnoticed. The classic symptoms are excessive thirst, excessive urination, excessive hunger, weight loss, and itching, especially of the genitals—but the problem is that only about half of maturity-onset diabetics have any of these symptoms; the disease is discovered accidentally in the course of a routine checkup or a medical examination for some other complaint. Too often, no diagnosis is made until some irreversible damage has been done. Don't think you're safe if you have an annual examination that includes a urinalysis, for the mild diabetic never has sugar in his urine and so the test only diagnoses cases that are relatively advanced.

If your chances of getting diabetes are high for reasons such as heredity, overweight, or having had several children—especially a larger-than-normal infant—ask your doctor to give you a glucose-tolerance test. This is a much more sensitive test than urinalysis and it can detect diabetes in a very early stage. Your best defense against the possible ravages of diabetes—severe cardiovascular disease, hypertension, strokes, unmanageable infections, blindness—is early diagnosis and treatment. And *with* early diagnosis, treatment is simple. Only about a quarter of maturity-onset diabetics have to use insulin; all the others can control the disease by diet alone or by the use of oral drugs. The use of oral drugs, however, is controversial, and if they are prescribed for you, you should get a second opinion, preferably from a diabetes specialist. The important thing to know is that diabetes *is* manageable, and that the maturity-onset diabetic who keeps his disease under control can lead a perfectly normal life, and live it just as fully as a nondiabetic.

The third area of health problems most often encountered in middle age involves changes in, or disorders of, the sex organs. Of these problems, the one that is best known, since it happens to every woman and every man hears about it, is menopause, the cessation of the menstrual flow. Actually, while this is the most obvious change that comes with the climacteric, there are others that precede menopause itself and involve a number of organs in the endocrine system, especially the hypothalamus, the pituitary, and the gonads. Some women, during their 40's, begin to experience hot flushes, emotional upsets, insomnia, weight gain, fatigue, vague aches and pains; other women never have any symptoms at all. While menopause can occur either earlier or later, it does so most commonly between the 46th and 50th years.

In almost all cases where the symptoms are severe enough to cause discomfort, they can be controlled by supplemental estrogen to replace that which the ovaries are ceasing to produce. It is most often taken in the form of one pill a day for three weeks out of every four. Some doctors recommend taking estrogen for just a year or two, or only as long as symptoms persist; others believe that post-menopausal women should take supplementary estrogen for the rest of their lives. Whether or not you take any medication, how much you take, and for how long are matters for you and your gynecologist to work out together, but the important thing to remember is that menopause is nothing to fear. If it causes any discomforts, they are now easy to deal with and your life should not be affected in any way whatsoever—except that at last you will be free of worries about conception and of the monthly bother of the menses.

A related matter of deep concern to middle-aging women and their husbands is the prospect of hysterectomy. It is not uncommon for women to begin having heavier than usual bleeding or even bouts of hemorrhaging during the premenopausal years. This is often due to hormone disturbances that can be controlled by medication, but a surprising number of doctors (most often surgeons, but even, occasionally, gynecologists) recommend hysterectomy as the quick solution to the problem. Their attitude is that when a woman is finished with child-bearing, her uterus is expendable. Dr. William A. Nolen, chief of the Department of Surgery at Meeker County Hospital in Litchfield, Minnesota, castigates this as "male chauvinism at its most flagrant." "A patient's ovaries," he adds, "are another favorite target of both gynecologists and general surgeons. There's a saying in surgical circles that if ovaries were testicles, there'd be a lot fewer of them removed. I know that's true."

So be careful. Before you agree to a hysterectomy, check with a second doctor—if possible, a gynecologist, since this is the specialist who can often control functional bleeding with medication. If, however, the bleeding cannot be controlled, if you have tumors so large that they are creating pressure on other organs, or if there is any possibility of cancer, then you should go ahead with the operation without delay—and without undue anxiety. The operation is not a particularly difficult one and it will not leave you altered in any important way. The incision can usually be made along the line of the pubic hair so that the scar is virtually invisible, and sometimes a hysterectomy can be performed through the vagina so that there is no scar at all. We have already pointed out that a hysterectomy does not affect sexual performance, but here is further word from an expert on the subject, Dr. Clarence J. Schein, professor of surgery at Albert Einstein College of Medicine, Montefiore Hospital and Medical Center in New York City: "Your sex life is unimpaired and may actually be improved, since you are free of the problems of pregnancy precautions. There is no impairment of any sexual function."

And as for ovaries, a cyst on an ovary can be dealt with by the removal of the cyst, but all too often it results in removal of the ovary, a simpler task for the surgeon. Of course, if there is cancer, the ovary has to go. If there is not, tell your doctor that you expect to come out of the operating room with the two ovaries you go in with—unless he can satisfactorily explain why it isn't possible..

Breast cancer is the other big worry of middle-aged women, and perhaps the most frightening one of all. And with some reason: it is the most common cancer that women get and accounts for 20 per cent of all female malignancies. Here again, early discovery and treatment will minimize the risks. In addition to your regular twice-a-year visits to the doctor (or even more frequent ones if recommended), you must go *at once* if you discover a lump. (Either your own doctor or your local branch of the American Cancer Society will show you how to examine yourself.) Breast cancer, if it is detected early—before it has spread into adjacent lymph nodes —is curable in 80 to 90 per cent of the cases.

It is a psychological shock to have a breast removed, but that is not nearly so serious as dying of cancer, and the early-detection recovery rate should be impressive enough to make any woman with a breast lump run, not walk, to her doctor. The number of women who have had mastectomies is large, and those who join their ranks soon learn that they look just the same in clothes or a bathing suit as they ever did, thanks to new jellylike prostheses that look, feel, and move so much like a real breast that no one except a husband or lover knows the difference. For many women, the hardest aspect of recovery from breast removal is the emotional one, but the American Cancer Society says that most of the emotional problems associated with mastectomy can be offset by rehabilitation. Toward this end, the A.C.S. operates a Reach to Recovery program that helps 30,000 patients a year throughout the country; volunteers who have made an excellent recovery, both physically and psychologically, from breast-removal operations, visit patients in the hospital and give them not only useful practical advice but invaluable psychological support.

Currently, there is a good deal of controversy about the preferred method of treatment of breast cancer. Some doctors favor a radical operation (which includes removal of some chest wall muscle and contents of the armpit), some remove just the breast, some remove the lump and leave the breast, some vary the treatment to fit the individual case. A number of doctors also use medication or X-ray treatments along with surgery part or all of the time. The choice of treatment depends on the patient's condition and on the individual doctor, and you yourself are probably not the best judge of what treatment you should have. You should, though, seek a second opinion unless you are convinced that your doctor is outstandingly qualified. The one thing you *can't* do is ignore a breast lump. Most of them turn out to be benign, but you have to find out. And fast. A delay in seeking treatment can make all the difference between life and death.

Male readers may be feeling ignored after this lengthy recital of female ills, but the fact is that aside from heart attack, men do not have as many ailments in middle age as women do. The most common one is prostatism, an obstruction of the bladder outlet caused by enlargement of the prostate gland. Enlargement of the gland is quite common; it is found in about 40 per cent of men beyond the age of 60, but it is not always severe enough to cause symptoms.

But when symptoms do occur, they are annoying rather than frightening, for they usually consist of urinary frequency, urinary urgency or burning, and, only in more advanced cases, difficult urination or a small and feeble stream. Such symptoms must not be ignored because the longer the condition is neglected, the more severe it is likely to become. Mild cases of prostatism can often be treated at home or in the doctor's office. More severe cases usually require surgical correction; when surgery is necessary, it should not be feared, for this operation is almost always completely successful and has no untoward side effects.

In most cases, only the overgrown portion of the gland that is causing an obstruction is removed. If the gland is found to be cancerous, however, then it must be removed in its entirety. There are several methods of performing the operation, and again, only the urologist or surgeon can decide which is correct for the particular case. The operation carries no special risks and in a healthy male complete convalescence requires only a few weeks.

What most men worry about, of course, is not typical postoperative complications but the effect of the operation on their sexual capacity and enjoyment. We said earlier that most prostatectomies diminish neither capacity nor enjoyment, and to reinforce this reassurance we quote Dr. Clarence J. Schein once more: "[After prostatectomy] sexual performance is not adversely affected. Those who were potent before remain so; those who were impotent before are not improved. The individual whose sexual powers were waning at the time of surgery may go either way . . . [but] sexual feeling and excitement are not altered in the potent individual."

Before we leave the realm of sexual problems, we might briefly explore those failures to function sexually that are not helped by the kind of home remedies outlined in Chapter 4. Although the symptoms are physical, their underlying causes are usually psychological, and they generally respond only to psychotherapy. Fortunately, in very recent years there have been major advances in sex therapy, and clinics offering different kinds of treatment exist in many cities.

For those couples whose sexual dysfunction is really severe, consisting of incomplete, abnormal, or impaired response to sexual stimulation, a professional treatment center should be considered. In the main, such centers claim to use programs based on the techniques originated by Dr. William Masters and Mrs. Virginia Johnson at the Reproductive Biology Research Foundation in St. Louis, where 80 per cent of their several thousands of patients have been treated successfully.

There are at least 3500—and possibly many more—such centers operating now in various parts of the country. Those that follow the Masters and Johnson program treat couples only and usually charge about $2500 for a two-week intensive treatment program with follow-up sessions later. Male and female co-therapists are employed to help the two partners understand the causes of each other's special problems (impotence, frigidity, premature or delayed ejaculation, painful intercourse, and the like) and to work with each other to overcome them by providing cooperation, support, and effective stimulation.

Other clinics or centers use different methods of many kinds, and their fees usually run upward from $40 an hour per couple (for ten to twenty hours). Some are affiliated with foundations, with public or semiprivate hospitals, or with public-health services; some are private money-makers. Some specialize in treating nonconventional couples such as homosexuals or the unmarried. Dr. Masters has warned, "The opportunities for charlatanism are abundant. Possibly 50 out of the more than 3000 [sexual treatment centers] might meet all standards of acceptability."

In their published writings and in their lectures, Masters and Johnson have reported on numerous cases, treated at their own clinic, in which the dispelling of false ideas about sex in middle age, the elimination of anxiety, the use of new and more effective stimulative techniques, and the administration of estrogen therapy (if needed) restored sexual function completely to couples in whom it had vanished. The major feature of the Masters and Johnson technique is a slow, step-by-step reconditioning that enables patients to enjoy sexual feelings by eliminating goals and hence the fear of failure to achieve them.

A typical case is that of a married couple who had an adequate, but not ideal, sex life for many years (the wife had orgasm only sometimes) until, at 61, the husband became impotent. They had been on a long trip during which, though tired from sight-seeing and traveling, he sought more sex than usual in a spirit of holiday fun. But due to fatigue, for the first time in his life he became keenly aware of the slowness of his responses; he began to worry, and the more he worried, the harder he tried—and the worse he got. At last he failed altogether, and after a few successive failures, gave up. When they got back home, he consulted his family physician, who assured him that impotence was normal in a man of 61, and that nothing could be done about it.

The man and his wife accepted this fate for five years; then, still hoping for help, they went to the Masters and Johnson clinic when he was 66 and she was 62. There they learned that slower responses are normal in middle-aged persons, that they could be compensated for by taking more time and paying more attention to techniques of arousal, and that it is of paramount importance not to try to force male response. In the course of a week of therapy and of sexual practice with his wife, the man lost his anxiety, regained his capacity to function, and the pair resumed their sex life. Following up six years later, Masters and Johnson found them still happily making love once or twice a week.

It is not feasible for every couple who seeks help to go to St. Louis but those who cannot should be able to find a good center, if not nearby, at least in their own part of the country. Masters and Johnson have actually trained twelve teams at their own foundation; five of them are still there and the other seven are practicing elsewhere. Their names and locations can be found in the notes to this chapter.

Take Dr. Masters' warning seriously, and if you decide to attend a treatment center, shop with extreme care. Without any other guidelines, it is probably safest to stick to those clinics that are connected with universities or reputable hospitals. You might also ask your local family agency affiliated with the Family Service Association of America for a recommendation.

Some of the better programs pay special attention to the sexual dysfunctions of middle age. One of these is at Long Island Jewish Hillside Medical Center, where the Program of Human Sexuality is headed by Dr. Leon Zussman and his wife Shirley, a marriage and family professor at New York's Finch College. This program holds special interest for the middle-aged because of its sharp focus on the "menopausal couple." While changes associated with the climacteric are taking place in the woman, Dr. Zussman says, "counseling of the menopausal couple can be very effective in opening new lines of communication and dispelling myths. At this time of life, when child-rearing is no longer paramount, a renewed interest in each other could make this one of the more satisfactory periods of a marital relationship. If you're going to retire you might as well retire into a good sex life as well as a good golf life." We certainly agree with Dr. Zussman's attitude.

If there is a chance that treatment in a sex-therapy clinic could make a major improvement in your life, and if you can afford it, you owe it to yourself to try it. People with deep-seated sex problems tend to avoid seeking treatment out of shame; their usual explanation is that it's hopeless anyway, but the data clearly show that it isn't usually so.

Not only does middle age impose on us some physical problems that we must deal with knowledgeably, but it also imposes on us problems arising from the infirmities of aging parents. In the last chapter we touched upon the need to adjust emotionally to our parents' increasing dependence. Here, we want to talk about the practical problems that often arise and what we can do to solve them. When aged parents become ill and unable to care for themselves, or if one of them is widowed and becomes too depressed to live alone, the middle-aged children are often forced to make decisions for them, or even to take over completely, and this can involve some painful burdens. The decision as to whether or not to take them into our own homes is one of the hardest of a lifetime— but to share our homes with relatives, especially ill, failing, or despondent parents, is virtually always a death-blow to the Prime Time way of life. Privacy, *joie de vivre*, spontaneity, vacationing, entertaining, every aspect of life is affected—adversely. Yet we have a clear duty and a need to do something. The question is, what?

The answer, essentially, is that we, the middle-aged children, should painstakingly investigate the other alternatives, offer our best judgment about them to our aging parents, help them make their own decision, and then assist them in putting that decision into effect. The choice of alternative will be determined, primarily, by the age and health of the parents and their financial resources. A simple and often workable solution for an elderly widow who is still in reasonably good physical health is to suggest that she share her home with a like person, perhaps an old friend who is in a similar situation. An aging widower who can't cook and keep house might find life in a men's residential club comfortable and congenial—if he can afford it.

For the aging couple with adequate savings, there are now retirement villages or communities in many parts of the country; you can find advertisements for them in newspapers and magazines.

They offer either condominium apartments or private houses in a completely cared for environment: the grass is cut, the snow shoveled, the gardens tended, the streets patrolled; there is swimming, golf, bus service to shopping and religious services; there is a recreation center where one can find partners for bridge, chess, or gin rummy; there are classes in art, sewing, assorted arts and crafts. There are often medical facilities on the premises, sometimes even a hospital, so that people who live in the community don't have to travel outside it for services unless they prefer to.

Within about a hundred miles of New York City, prices of houses or apartments in the more desirable retirement communities start at about $25,000 and rise to well over double that. In addition, there are monthly mortgage payments and upkeep or membership charges that can easily total several hundred dollars a month. In some other areas, such as Florida, the starting prices are considerably lower.

But clearly, such facilities are for the still active and the comparatively affluent only—and for those who like them. Many an aging man or woman, even though able to afford it, would find such a community unacceptable; they feel that the absence of children or young couples seems unnatural and depressing and creates an atmosphere of a place where old folks wait to die.

Yet for many others, the country-club atmosphere of the retirement village seems like nirvana after a lifetime of hard work, and they enjoy the companionship of others their own age, the freedom from chores, and the assurance that they will be cared for if they fall ill, and will have companionship if their spouse dies.

Whether old persons are better off in age-segregated communities of this sort or in mixed communities is a matter of controversy. One person who believes that the age-homogeneous community is better, and who brings some evidence to the debate, is Dr. Arlie Russell Hochschild, a sociologist at the University of California at Berkeley. Dr. Hochschild studied the residents of Merrill Court, a small apartment house in the San Francisco area which is occupied exclusively by 37 aged women and 6 aged men. All 43 are fundamentalist, conservative, of Mid- or Southwestern origin, from the blue-collar economic class, and they range in age from the 60's into the 80's. Although each apartment in Merrill Court has its own kitchen, life there in many ways resembles that in a commune. The younger, healthier individuals take care of the older, sicker ones, and there are strong social ties. There are numerous get-togethers which revolve around coffee parties, lunches, and exchanges of homemade food and potted plants. Dr. Hochschild finds this a highly successful community because the members have a great deal in common and form very close friendships. They are never isolated and they have the mutual satisfaction of being helpful to each other. Because they are not dependent on their families, they are able to maintain strong connections with their children and grandchildren. All in all, it is undoubtedly a splendid solution to a lonely old age for these particular people, but clearly, it wouldn't suit everybody.

More conventional and more broadly acceptable are the non-profit life-care centers run by churches, unions, or other organizations. In these, residents have single or double rooms with or without private bath, and are served their meals in dining rooms. There are public rooms, recreational facilities, libraries, and medical care. The new resident pays an entrance fee, a monthly maintenance fee, and in addition agrees to leave his entire estate to the organization. Costs at such centers vary widely, as do their facilities, clientele, food, ambience, and medical care. In the main, they are a good buy.

Do be certain, however, before you sign any papers turning over an estate to an organization, that its credentials are impeccable. A good way to check is through the families of a few patients who have already been in residence for some time.

The most publicized and certainly the most widely used form of old-age residence is the nursing home. There are about 23,000 of them in the United States and they are largely supported by public funds. Of the $4.5 billion that was spent in nursing homes in 1973, half came from the federal government and 25 to 30 per cent more from state and local funds. There are presently more than 20 million Americans over the age of 65, and a third of these are over 75; it is this third that accounts for most nursing-home patients.

Many old people who are confined to wheelchairs or bed, or require complex nursing care for other reasons, wind up in nursing homes because, in most cases, there is no other solution. Private nursing care is beyond the means of all but the very wealthy, but in a nursing home Medicare and Medicaid are available to pay the bills. It works like this: when the doctor in charge deems that a patient does not need hospitalization but only nursing care, Medicare will pay for such care in a nursing home (for persons over 65) for a limited number of days. After that time, the patient must pay his own bills until he runs out of money, or until he *almost* does. This doesn't take long for most people, since nursing-home rates run from a usual minimum of $150 a week in rural areas to several hundred a week in more affluent and expensive urban areas. These fees do not include such items as clothing, laundry, medication, doctors' visits, and personal purchases or expenses. But when the patient's savings are gone, then Medicaid comes to the rescue and pays all the bills thenceforward.

The precise point at which it does so varies from state to state, since Medicaid is a matching-funds program run jointly by the federal government and the states, and the regulations governing requirements for aid differ among the latter. In New York, Medicaid takes over when the individual is down to $1750 (or $2500 for a couple), but in some states he is not eligible for Medicaid until he has no resources at all. This is extremely degrading to those people who have always wanted to be sure of a decent funeral, or to whom it is meaningful to buy presents for members of the family on special occasions.

Eligibility for Medicaid has no relationship to the amount of money the applicants' children earn or have. In practice, even well-to-do families who would ordinarily shun any form of "charity" usually resort to Medicaid if their parents live for a long time, because the bills commonly run to more than $1000 a month and very few families can afford such a drain over a period of years. The vast majority of nursing-home patients are on Medicaid and since we and our parents all contributed the tax money to make it possible, you should not feel embarrassed or ashamed if your parents take advantage of it.

The problem, then, isn't money. The problem is that by now we have all been let in on the nasty secret that most nursing homes are degrading, filthy, understaffed, inhuman, money-oriented institutions. Many have made exorbitant profits by bilking patients in various ways. A common one is to withhold the $30-a-month personal allowance Medicaid patients are entitled to; this is a simple matter since both Medicaid and Social Security checks are usually cashed by the home, and if the patient is senile, acutely ill, or simply ignorant of his rights, the home keeps the $30. Another profit-maker is cutting the food budget; it is not too difficult to show a reasonable daily cost for food on the books while actually spending half of that and feeding patients a bare subsistence diet. The worst abuse of all is getting the senile or unwary patient to sign away his assets without knowing what he is signing. We have all read about these scandals—so how can you put your parents into such a place? You can't, of course. What other choice do you have? Only one. You have to find a *good* nursing home. It isn't easy, but it can be done.

Your task will be much simpler if you start before you have to, so that you have all the time you need. If your parent is in declining health or hospitalized, begin to make inquiries at once. The best nursing homes are usually the nonprofit ones and they always have the longest waiting lists, so put your name on a list or two before you do anything else; you can always take it off later if you want to.

If you possibly can, visit three or four (or even five or six) nursing homes and stay for a couple of hours each time. If the management is reluctant to let you stay that long, it's probably the wrong place.

Go to dining rooms, craft rooms, patients' rooms; many patients, especially those who are bedridden, will be delighted to have company and will welcome your visit. Notice whether or not the patient is clean, and use your nose. Talk to as many patients as you can and keep your eyes and ears wide open. The difference between a hostile or indifferent staff and a caring and attentive one is not hard to detect if you pay attention to small interchanges.

Inspect the bathrooms, whether private or common. Ask to visit the kitchen, too, and if you are favorably impressed with what you see, try to stay on as a paying guest for lunch or dinner. Both the quality of the meal and the mood of the diners should tell you a good deal.

All nursing homes are inspected regularly, and reports are on file in your state; call your state Department of Health and ask where the Medicare and Medicaid reports can be inspected. It is your legal right to see them.

When you have narrowed your choice to two or three homes, it would be wise to discuss the matter with your parent (assuming that he or she is compos mentis and able to do so). It might be a good idea to present a few pictures of the homes and describe them in detail, so that your parent has some voice in making the decision and doesn't feel totally powerless. Playing even a small role in the decision-making can do much to ease the change to institutional living and to leave the patient with some sense of dignity and self-respect.

Yet the truth is that no matter how carefully you choose, or how good the home is, it is going to be a shock for your parent at first. The period of adjustment may be nearly as difficult for you as for the patient: you will undoubtedly hear a large number of complaints in the first weeks, and you will surely be sympathetic and troubled. But try not to panic; not yet. Investigate specific complaints to find out if they are legitimate and if you can do anything about them. If the complaints are vague, the trouble may be something your parent isn't expressing—a sense of loneliness or inadequate social contact, or a sense of hopelessness and boredom because there is nothing to do. It is highly important that all nursing-home patients who are able have scheduled activities and plenty of opportunity to socialize. If they can't find friends within the walls, it might be the best institution in the area but the wrong one for your parent. If, on the other hand, your parent *does* fit into the nursing-home environment by making friends quickly, your troubles are virtually over.

Bernice comments

I have never had the problem of moving a parent into a nursing home but I did have exactly the same kind of experience with an aunt. My father's sister, Anne, an elderly spinster, had lived for a number of years with a girlhood friend who had been widowed at an early age. Aunt Anne was an uncommonly independent, strong woman who, well after her 70th birthday, was still working full time as secretary to the president of a small corporation. It came as a rude shock to everyone when she suffered a slight stroke in her mid-70's, fell, and shattered the bones in her right arm. She was hospitalized for several weeks but by the time she was discharged, she was apparently fine and returned to her home. Almost immediately afterward, however, she had several fainting spells, and the doctor thought it likely that she was having a series of small strokes; although she suffered no impairment, it was obvious that she could not be left alone even for short periods.

At first it looked as if the problem could easily be solved by hiring a daily companion, but then Aunt Anne's roommate, Mrs. C., confided to me that she was afraid to go to sleep at night for fear that Anne would fall again and be hurt. I realized that of course Mrs. C. ought not to be burdened with this responsibility and because I was the relative in charge, a sort of surrogate daughter, I began to make inquiries about nursing homes.

Aunt Anne was fully aware of the situation, and since not going to work for the first time in her adult life made her days intolerably dull, she was interested in, and even mildly enthusiastic about, the possibility of moving into what she hoped would be a livelier and more stimulating place. I lived in Manhattan at that time and my aunt in a suburb, and we both concluded that since I would surely be her most frequent visitor, I should look for a nursing home in Manhattan. There were several homes that were brand-new; they were clean, attractive, well-appointed, bustling with starch-crisp nurses, and they all looked fine to me. Since my aunt had a comfortable bank account and could afford to pay top rates after the allowed 100 days of Medicare benefits, I selected, with her approval, what I thought was the best of the lot.

On moving day, Aunt Anne seemed to have lost most of her earlier interest and replaced it with palpable anxiety. By the time we arrived at the home she looked frankly depressed and frightened. She dutifully admired the lovely gardens and her charming room, yet all the time I was reminded of a terrified but game child arriving at camp for the first time and trying to make a good show of it. I promised to visit every day for a while and to take her out to lunch often, and that seemed to cheer her up just a trifle.

The next day when I arrived, the sad little-girl look was gone and in its place was righteous wrath. "What kind of place is this, anyway?" my aunt stormed. "You led me to believe that I was going to a nursing home. This is no nursing home, it's a mental hospital! Everybody here is crazy! I haven't gotten a single appropriate answer from anybody I've spoken to and *you take me out of here right now!*" Alas, everything she said was true. Taken in by all the flowers, the pretty wallpaper, and the charming curtains and bedspreads, I had not asked to visit *all* the floors, and had seen only those the administrator chose to show me. Yes, this floor was for patients who were mentally disturbed, and no, my aunt certainly did not belong there, but at the present time it was the only room available. I rushed out and spent the next days making arrangements for a move to another nursing home.

The second home looked much like the first, but this time, I made certain that my aunt would have people to talk to. She shared a large and attractive room with a lovely woman—who turned out to be totally incontinent. The floor of the room and its private bathroom were frequently dotted with puddles which no one hurried to clean up; the odor became offensive and the slippery floors were hazardous as well. I began to shop again, slowly and carefully.

By now, I had learned quite a bit, all of it the hard way, and at $1400 a month, Aunt Anne's bank account was rapidly dwindling. One of the things I had learned in my willy-nilly course of study was that for patients who could pay, immediate openings were far more plentiful than for Medicaid patients, since at least in New York, Medicaid pays the homes a somewhat lower rate than private patients do. But once a patient is installed, the changeover to Medicaid status takes place automatically when the patient becomes eligible for it. So I couldn't waste too much time because I was in a race against the bank book; I had to get Aunt Anne into the right place while she could still pay; besides, all of this shifting around was upsetting to me and much more so to my aunt. Following the tennis adage, "Always change a losing game," I cast about for some days for a way to change it. And then it came to me in a flash. Why was I trying to keep her in the city, where everything is crowded and expensive? Why not try a suburban home? I went back to Aunt Anne's old neighborhood and found exactly the right place. As soon as we began to drive through the old well-known streets her eyes lit up for the first time in months. And when we entered the lobby and she saw a familiar face, I knew that if only I had managed to check *all* of the variables this time, we had it made.

Aunt Anne stayed in that nursing home, busy and apparently quite content, until her death several years later. She had what seemed to be vast numbers of friends, and on many of my visits she covertly peeked at her watch hoping that I wouldn't make her late for her next activity. She studied oil and watercolor painting and turned out to be surprisingly good at both. Her paintings were exhibited in the lobby and she was as proud as if it had been a Madison Avenue gallery. Having always been enthusiastic about knitting and crocheting, she soon gained a reputation as the expert in residence and enjoyed teaching many of her fancy stitches to other women. And she even had a couple of elderly "gentlemen callers" who came by wheelchair to visit or to escort her to dinner or an evening's entertainment.

When Aunt Anne's money ran out and she went on Medicaid, we were both surprised and grateful to learn that its provisions included hairdressing service once a week, a stipend to pay for the purchase of small items and for dry cleaning (which was not done on the premises), and a free account for all supplies in the arts and crafts room.

It was not the very best of all possible worlds, to be sure. In another time, another place, Aunt Anne would have lived out her days more normally and perhaps more satisfyingly in the bosom of an extended family. Under the contemporary and personal circumstances, that was simply not possible—but the solution we found was not a bad one. She *was* left with her dignity and a sense of importance within her small world, and not only did the family visit her often, but the people she lived with became a kind of family to her too.

It makes little sense to ponder what would have been possible in some other time. The problems that arise now have to be dealt with in the context of now. We can deal fairly well with those problems, whether they involve ourselves or our parents, provided we learn what to expect, how to face the realities as they materialize, and, above all, how to cope with them through informed and appropriate action.

8 *The Phoenix from the Ashes*

THE POSSIBILITIES OF
THE GOOD LIFE IN MIDDLE AGE,
DESPITE DIVORCE OR WIDOWHOOD

For some of them, the worst time is late afternoon, when they come home and open the door to the dead stillness inside, or feel the approach of evening and night, and the aloneness, as something malevolent enveloping and smothering them.

For some, the worst time is any holiday or anniversary, when the air that once was filled with glad greetings and toasts is leaden and silent, the coffee table on which gifts were exchanged and excitedly unwrapped is bare. Visions of bygone celebrations obscure the book one is doggedly trying to read; then the grief so slowly mastered rises up suddenly and unexpectedly in one's throat, scalding and bitter.

For some, the worst time is a visit to married friends, a meal alone in a restaurant—any time, indeed, when one sees couples talking to each other and looking at each other in that special, belonging way that makes one's own singleness feel as noticeable and grotesque as the stump of an amputated arm.

We have made it clear throughout this book that many of the potential rewards of the New Middle Age come from the postparental couple's regained intimacy, increased leisure, greater financial freedom, and heightened sharing of new experience. But what if, in middle life, the marriage is broken by divorce or death, and each partner is suddenly a bleeding and dismembered half of what was so long whole? How, then, can they experience middle age as anything but a partial death, an exile, a gray succession of unwanted days and wasted time?

183

Those who come to middle age without ever having been married—roughly one out of every twenty males and females—are not likely to perceive it in this fashion; they long ago made a different bargain with life than those who married, and in middle age look for a continuation of that bargain. Some of the advantages of the New Middle Age apply to them, but many others do not; the matter, however, lies outside the scope of this book.

But the vast majority of those who arrive at middle age married, and then find themselves single again, still want what *they* had long ago bargained for, namely, the daily experience of life as a *not-alone*, a *together*, a two-person entity—the complete creature who, in Plato's charming fable, was split into two halves by the gods, and each half of which has ever since sought to be whole again. While the divorced and the widowed are psychologically dissimilar in many ways, they are similar in this most fundamental one: formerly they were complete and now are partial—and they find it alien, uncongenial, and unnatural.

There are, however, major differences in the two kinds of partner loss, and we will therefore look at them separately, taking the lesser disaster, divorce, first. The divorce rate has been rising steadily since 1962, continuing the long-range trend of more than a hundred years. It has risen for the middle-aged as well as the young: roughly twice as many middle-aged people (nearly 4 per cent of all middle-aged males and somewhat over 5 per cent of all middle-aged females) are currently divorced as were a generation ago. Actually, the chance of divorce in middle age is a good deal higher than these figures suggest, for they show only how many were *divorced and still unremarried* at the time of the census. Since roughly one quarter of all marriages now end in divorce, and since nearly a quarter of those divorces occur after fifteen or more years of marriage, there must be something like a one-in-sixteen chance that a husband and wife now entering middle age will end up in divorce court.

The divorces of the young have a wide variety of well-known causes, but a great many of the divorces of the middle-aged have the same underlying cause: dissimilar development of the partners. We begin our young marriages expecting to remain suited to each other, but this expectation has no sound basis. As anthropologist Paul Bohannan says, in *Divorce and After,* "No one, at the time of marriage, can know what the spouse is going to become ... [or] what he himself may become." The insecure young man may have turned into an aggressive, self-confident success, while his bright, creative, worldly young wife may have become a fussy, compulsive homemaker; the bossy, critical young man may have remained bossy and critical while his passive young wife has completed her studies, made headway in a career, and become a stronger and more self-respecting person. The good fit is gone; now there is a poor fit, a continual clashing of gears. The spouses who once felt so ideally suited to each other now find one another hostile and cruel, or remote and cold, or simply (and worst of all) boring. They may not notice their mismatch until the children leave home; then, however, their teamwork as parents ends, and they rather abruptly become aware of how meaningless or even painful their relationship has become.

"Has become." The words are crucial, for a middle-age marriage that ends in divorce need not be accounted a total failure; it may have been a genuine success for many years, and only become a failure as time and circumstances caused the partners to become unmatched. But why not then accept what time has brought, and continue the marriage out of what was good in the past? Why not agree to coexist in peace and partnership, even if not in love and joy?

That, indeed, was the solution chosen a generation ago by the great majority of middle-aged people with deteriorated marriages. But with the advent of the New Middle Age, it is becoming less and less the solution of choice. The years of mid-life are now too many, too full of promise, to be wasted, and a marriage that has become unrewarding or unsatisfying is a poisoned milieu in which the partners wither and shrivel rather than flourish and expand.

We are certainly not suggesting that every middle-aged couple whose marriage is less than ideal ought to be divorced, for the psychic and practical costs of divorce are very high, and a marriage that is less than ideal may still be relatively good and an adequate basis for the Prime Time way of life. We are, however, suggesting —in fact, asserting—that a relationship which is revealed, in the postparental period, as having grown hopelessly distant or con-flict-ridden is bound to prevent both partners from getting any-thing but the merest fringe benefits of the New Middle Age. If such a marriage cannot be reconstructed—and only a minority can—then the one chance for the partners to make good on the promise of modern mid-life is to subject themselves to the agonizing process of divorce, and for both to make a determined search, despite the expected disappointments and obstacles, for the mates they now need.

In focusing on the positive and creative potential of divorce, we are not ignoring its negative and destructive aspects. To nearly all who undergo it, it is disorienting, shocking, embarrassing, and frightening, and some divorced people are so damaged as to remain emotionally and socially crippled for life. But the great majority are galvanized by divorce into rebuilding their lives and they gain room for personal growth far beyond that which had taken place within the constrictions of the marital relationship. Divorce is, in sum, both a violent wound and a cure, the shattering of a way of life and the opportunity to build a better one, an exile and yet a liberation.

Morton comments

Some years ago, in connection with a book I was writing on divorce *(The World of the Formerly Married)*, I interviewed some 200 people and conducted a questionnaire survey of nearly 400 others; since then, in connection with other work, I have interviewed many hundreds more. Of them all, I can recall only a handful who did not suffer considerable pain as a result of the marital breakup; many suffered intensely, some to the point of attempting suicide. But on the other hand, I can recall very few who, either immediately or after a while, did not also consider themselves better off and happier than they had been toward the end of the marriage. The most nearly typical experience right after the breakup of marriage seemed to be a bewildering mixture of sorrow and relief, a vacillation between gloom and optimism, an alternation of feeling terrible and feeling very good. Even those who were most grieved and distraught were surprised by their frequent moods of expansiveness and euphoria;

but even those who were happiest to be free of the marriage were astonished to find themselves frequently feeling desolate and cast out. This mixture of moods changed with time: as they grew accustomed to thinking of themselves as single, learned to take care of themselves alone, and discovered their capacity for entering into new relationships, they suffered less, ceased to mourn, and increasingly experienced feelings of achievement and growth. Aside from a small minority, they approved of the changes in themselves that had taken place since their divorce, and looked back with embarrassment or pity on the persons they had been in their faulty marriages.

I myself felt just such an alternation of moods during my first experience of separation. (I have been divorced twice, once at 44 and once at 51.) Even though I had long sought the first separation and was intensely relieved when it was finally a *fait accompli,* many a time during my first two years of single life I would feel something close to panic. Isolated in my little apartment, I would cling to the telephone as to a lifeline; I would spend interminable evenings with women I found boring or disagreeable rather than be alone. But in those same years I also saw myself changing in ways that I found deeply gratifying. I made a pleasant home for myself in the city, and an even pleasanter one in the country; I became competent at running my two homes, taking care of my own needs, and being a good host to my friends; I learned to move easily and with a fair degree of self-confidence among other unmarried people; I explored my own intellectual, emotional, and sexual capacities. It seemed to me after a while that in considerable part I was no longer the person I had formerly been—and I much preferred the new one to the old. And even though I expected from the outset that I would eventually remarry, and after some years very much wanted to do so, I never regretted the divorce and felt that even if I lived out my life alone as the person I had become, I would have had the better of it.

The things the divorced learn about themselves, and the growth they experience, are positive gains for them even if they never remarry, and even if they remarry unsuccessfully. I know, because I myself remarried after five years of bachelorhood, and suspected even during the honeymoon that I had wishfully ignored traits in my wife that presaged intolerable conflicts; stubbornly, I tried for two years to make the marriage work, then could stand it no longer. But depressing as it was to have to uproot myself again, I lost little by it psychologically, for this time I felt no need to rediscover, rebuild, and expand myself as I had the first time. I was who I was, and I still approved of myself.

Had there been no Bernice, I would have begun to search for another someone. But she, beginning to recover from the death of her husband, invited me, her old friend, to dinner as an act of charity and let me talk about my troubles. A few days later I took her to dinner and let her talk about her late husband, David (who had been my dear friend). We found comfort in each other, and in a matter of weeks, when we no longer needed comforting, were astonished to find that we had become knitted together by our common interests, long knowledge of each other, mutual respect and admiration, and a new addition, physical attraction. After only a short time, we knew that we loved each other, and said so. And this time I knew before we were married, and have known every day of the years since then, that I had found the real fit, the other half of the self I had become.

Despite the potential rewards divorce offers to those whose marriages have become moribund and meaningless, such people —especially if they are already middle-aged—are generally filled with apprehension at the very thought of trying to dissolve their marriages. For one thing, they are afraid that the psychological and social costs of divorce, as well as the financial ones, may be more than they can stand; for another, they feel that their chances of finding a new and more suitable partner are small or even nil. Yet in many ways divorce for the middle-aged is a good deal less hazardous or difficult than it used to be—and far less so than it is for most younger people.

A decade or two ago, the middle-aged woman facing divorce was often terrified at the prospect of being abandoned to fend for herself on a mere pittance. In most cases, such alimony as she received would enable her to barely get by; as for supplementing it by earnings of her own, if she was a middle-aged housewife she had neither marketable skills nor any confidence that she could acquire them. And like as not, she still had one or two children in school for whom she had to maintain a home. Today, as we have already noted, children are generally on their own by the time the mother is middle-aged—and she, in most cases, has worked in the past, has been working in recent years, or has multiple opportunities for training in new skills. The middle-aged woman facing divorce today, in short, is unlikely to be in serious financial difficulty, even if she receives little or no alimony.

At the same time, this development is making divorce for middle-aged men less financially crippling than it used to be. The changes in woman's status and opportunities over the past generation, since the advent of the women's liberation movement, have made some women reject alimony, and made many divorce-court judges alter their attitudes toward it. According to Philip F. Solomon, president of the American Academy of Matrimonial Lawyers, instead of viewing alimony as a punishment of the husband (who, by convention, generally assumes the role of the "guilty" party), judges are more often making monetary awards on the basis of provable need on the wife's part, taking into account her ability to earn part or all of her own living.

Dividing the possessions was always an area of struggle and suffering for the divorcing couple. Emotionally, it may still be as difficult as ever, but at least in practical terms it is somewhat easier for the middle-aged than formerly, again because they arrive at the postparental phase of life earlier. The oversized house or apartment is no longer needed, and giving it up and dividing its contents is not only feasible but avoids the expulsion of one partner or the other (usually the husband), possessionless, into the dreary limbo of sublet rooms and third-rate residential hotels.

Dividing up the children—or, more precisely, dealing with details of child support, custody, visitation rights, summer plans, education and medical questions, and the like—is the "most enduring pain of divorce," according to Professor Bohannan. But not for the middle-aged. At most, they have only a few years until their children are no longer minors and no longer a source of involvement and conflict between the ex-spouses. Nowadays, in fact, by age 18 most children live away from home and are scarcely subject to parental control. In sum, for those whose marriages break up in middle age, this most enduring pain of divorce, if it exists at all, is no longer enduring.

Socially, the divorced person was a virtual pariah earlier in the century; even a generation ago, divorce carried something of a stigma in many small communities and in some social circles even in big cities. But it has become very much more acceptable since then, and today few men or women feel much discomfort at being identified as divorced. The change has been particularly noteworthy for the middle-aged. Divorce in mid-life used to be viewed as not just wrong but ridiculous; as middle age has come, however, to be less a time of stagnation and retreat, and more a time of second flowering, acceptance of and respect for the divorcing middle-aged person have grown.

That former intolerance probably owed much to the discomfort many people felt at the thought of middle-aged men and women "dating" and having sexual alliances. Such things, if not downright immoral, were regarded as unnatural and unseemly at their age. But as national attitudes toward middle age have changed and sexual activity in married middle-aged people has come to seem natural and proper, it has come to seem equally so in postmarital middle-aged people.

The divorced themselves are often uncertain, at first, as to how well they will function sexually with new partners—particularly if, being middle-aged, they have long had sex with only one person. In actual fact, they tend to do rather well. Middle-aged divorced women, reports Dr. Paul Gebhard, director of the Institute for Sex Research, are distinctly more successful at achieving orgasm in their postmarital coitus than are younger divorced women; two thirds of those in the 41-to-45 age group, for instance, have orgasm 90 to 100 per cent of the time, as against only a little over half of those in the 31-to-35 group. We know of no comparable figures as to the potency of middle-aged divorced men, but our impression, from wide reading and interviewing, is that while many of them are often anxious about their ability to perform, they have potency difficulties only when the anxiety level is particularly high, as for instance in the first intimacies with a new partner. In general, however, most middle-aged divorced men experience a revival and intensification of their sexual drive; this is due in part to novelty, but in part to the discovery of a capacity for sexual pleasure that had either never been fully developed within the marital relationship or had been lost along the way.

In any case, although many middle-aged men and women fear, in advance of divorce, that they will fail to find sexual partners, their fears are largely groundless. Such survey data as exist, plus the evidence of interviews and firsthand observations, make it apparent that nearly all divorced males and females of middle age do find sexual partners—sometimes more would-be partners than they want—and do have sexual relations as often, and as successfully, as married persons of their own age.

But what most of them want even more is a genuinely intimate love relationship. Love in middle age used to be a topic for humor and satire; today, it is seen as a legitimate and admirable thing. The middle-aged divorced person seeks as eagerly as any young person to find someone to fall in love with, to share things with, to come home to. Where the middle-aged differ from the young in that search is in having more human experience to go on. They know more about themselves, about the complexities and realities of love, about what qualities they need in someone else and what they can give to someone else. All of which makes them more skittish than the young, more apt to back off cautiously from many a developing relationship. Yet at the same time they are driven on by the habits and hungers of their many years as part of a sexual-emotional companionship, and by their deep need to belong, to share, to be once again part of a completed pair.

Some never do achieve that goal. A few divorced people live out their years contentedly in the single state; far more of the unre-married make do, adjusting to their state as best they can, or slowly growing embittered, lonely, and discontented. Overall, the life-survival chances of the unremarried divorced person are lower than those of the married: suicide rates are at least three times as high for divorced women as for married women, and over four times as high for divorced men as for married men; admission rates for outpatient psychiatric services (in clinics of all sorts) are over five times as high for separated and divorced persons as for married persons of the same age; and in general, the life expectancy of all unmarried people (single, widowed, and divorced) is some five years less than that of the married. The difference in life expectancy, it used to be thought, meant only that psychologically ailing people, whose life chances were not as good as those of healthy people, were also more likely not to stay married, or not to marry at all. However, a new analysis of the data shows that this is not the case. Sociologist Walter R. Gove says that what accounts, in far larger part, for the longer life of the married is the "protective" nature of the marriage interaction; that is, the nurturance, care, and attention the partners provide each other. It is for such reasons that Dr. Alex Comfort urges those who remain single in middle age and later to consider doubling up with a friend of the same sex long before the onset of retirement and infirmity—to adopt, as he puts it, a "workable defensive posture" against the undue risks of living alone as one gets older.

By far the larger number of divorced persons, however, including those of middle age, do remarry. The proportion of the divorced who do so has been rising for several decades, and currently stands at about four fifths of all divorced women and over four fifths of all divorced men. Not surprisingly, the chances of remarriage are highest for the youngest, but according to calculations made for us by Arthur J. Norton of the Bureau of the Census, even for those who get divorced between 40 and 45 the chance of remarriage is three out of five for women and three out of four for men.

To be sure, what matters is not how many remarry, but how many remarry successfully. Some Freudian psychoanalysts maintain that without psychotherapy the divorced are certain to make exactly the same mistake again and again in choosing a mate; Dr. Edmund Bergler, for one, expounded that thesis in his book *Divorce Won't Help*. But sociologist Jessie Bernard and others, studying broader samples than psychoanalysts see, disagree. Only the minority, they hold, are neurotic and chronic failures at marriage; the majority learn by experience and therefore do better in their second marriages than in their first ones. After all, 100 per cent of the first marriages of divorced people did end in divorce, while at least half and possibly three quarters of their second marriages last the rest of their lives. Furthermore, roughly seven out of eight remarriages, in a survey made by Dr. Bernard, were rated anywhere from satisfactory to extremely satisfactory, and among a large group of remarried divorced women studied by sociologist William Goode, nearly nine out of ten regarded their second marriages as much better than their first ones.

It is true that the percentage of second marriages that break up is higher than the percentage of first marriages that do so, but in large part this is the result of experience rather than chronic marital incompetence. The divorced-and-remarried are quicker to recognize hopeless situations, and less fearful of taking drastic action, than people in first marriages. The higher risk of divorce in remarriages, however, probably does not apply to those who remarry in middle age, since so many of the problems that plague younger remarrying people—visitation rights, stepchild-stepparent relationships, and the like—do not exist for them.

But to speak of successful remarriage in middle age solely in terms of the problems that are minimal in it, or of the chance that it will last the rest of one's life, is not to convey its special quality. For it possesses a unique combination of attributes: intimacy combined with outgoingness, peacefulness combined with excitement, contentment combined with expansiveness. We have asked a number of people in successful middle-aged remarriages to tell us what is special about them, and they have replied in terms of love, mutual understanding, tolerance, shared enthusiasms, the expansion of interests and activities, the greater ability to talk out differences and disagreements, the satisfactions of mature sexual expression. After listening to all this attentively, and observing a number of such marriages over a long time, we would sum up the successful remarriage in middle age as a *benign environment.* It is like a sunny, sheltered, well-watered, and well-fertilized spot into which are transplanted shrubs that had been struggling along in a poor location but which now send out new shoots, put forth dense foliage, and are soon covered with blossoms.

So it is with two persons who transplant themselves into a good marriage in middle age; they become vital and luxuriant as they never could have been in the poisoned soil of the old marriage or the barren ground of the single life.

Two brief examples will illustrate the two different ways in which divorce, in middle age, can be compatible with—or even essential to—the pursuit of the Prime Time way of life.

Nancy J.'s story is far from ideal in outcome thus far—but it is also far from ended. Long locked in a frustrating, combative marriage, Nancy fought to break away after the children were grown, and finally obtained a divorce eight years ago. Financially, she has been hard pressed ever since; she gets very little alimony, and although she works she earns relatively little. She is quite attractive, but is now in her mid-50's, an age at which there are far fewer single men than single women. She has spent periods of many months during which either no men came her way or those who did wanted nothing but quick and uninvolved sex. She had one long passionate affair, but the man was intellectually far inferior to her and socially an oaf; for years she waited for him to get his own divorce—and only then admitted to herself that she and he were fundamentally incompatible, and that she could not marry him. At the moment, she is alone, and desperately unhappy.

For all that, Nancy has never regretted her own divorce. An artist, she studied book designing after leaving her husband and has been building a career which has brought her great satisfaction even if not much money so far. She has come to see herself in a new light, as a gifted and competent human being; at the same time, she has discovered in herself emotional and sexual capabilities that the marital relationship had never called forth. She has not yet made her middle age into what she wants it to be, but she knows now that the possibility exists. We, as her friends, worry about her and are grieved by her unfulfilled yearning to love and be loved, but each of us knew her as she was in her marriage and we have no doubt that even in her present incompleteness she is a more complete person, and even in her present discontent a more contented person, than she used to be.

Rudy A.'s story has a happier ending. Though long married to a domineering and belittling woman, he resisted divorce when she sought it because his fear of being single was stronger than his pain. At 52 he finally yielded, and found himself cast adrift and without any sense of direction. Lonely, unhappy, and feeling old and undesirable, he forced himself to make the rounds of the single world and to go out with women; but time and again he shied away in alarm from one or another of them, for they nearly all seemed to him to have some of the same tendencies that he had found so insufferable in his wife. The few who did not were far younger than he, but while he liked their less aggressive ways (and their youthful figures), he found them boring—and sensed that they found him stodgy and elderly.

Then five years ago, he met Stephanie. She was nearly his own age, and good-looking in a robust, chunky way. Age and robustness notwithstanding, she was also fluttery, indecisive, and clinging; she tended to lean on him as if he were a tower of strength—which made him feel more the man than he had in many years. That, and other things, made them fall in love in a matter of weeks.

We both remember them as they were at that time—a fond, clinging pair of lovers, he graying, she a bit broad of beam and well rounded both fore and aft, yet the two of them looking sweetly happy and not in the least foolish as they wandered down the beach, each with an arm around the other's waist. In their marriage, she has made him feel strong and decisive, and he has made her feel adorable and protected. More than that, he has made her feel talented, for while she had always been interested in antiques, it was not until he gave her strong backing and encouragement that she finally opened a tiny shop and discovered how good her taste was. Rudy, proud of her, has been assisting her on weekends, leaving the selection of purchases to her and concentrating for his part on restoration and repairs. He plans, in fact, to help her expand the shop and to join her in it full time when next year, at 60, he becomes eligible for retirement.

Retirement? Yes, but only from his long-time job. Rudy and Stephanie are the antithesis of the conventional retirement couple: what with the new business, their regular buying trips, and a wide circle of friends, their life has expanded rather than contracted. Their marriage is not, of course, all sweetness and light, and they do clash sometimes, but Stephanie usually gives way and then redresses the balance through artful cajoling. That may be an old-fashioned prefeminist method of dealing with marital conflicts, but it works for them. Such a marriage might function poorly or not at all during the child-rearing period, when there are so many other demands upon each partner; at the stage of life that Rudy and Stephanie have reached, however, it has proven nearly ideal for both of them, and is the very foundation upon which they have built a middle age that seems to them, in many ways, the best time of their lives.

Less common than divorce but usually exceeding it in its traumatic effects is the death of a spouse. And harsh and unpleasant though the reality is, there is no escaping it: dissolution of marriage through death, especially the death of a husband, is very much a fact of middle-aged life. According to *Current Population Reports* (1972) of the U.S. Bureau of the Census, there are close to 2 million widowers in the United States (2.9 per cent of the entire male population over the age of 18), but nearly 10 million widows (13.4 per cent of all adult women). If we look at the percentages of persons who are widowers and widows in each age group, we get a clearer idea of just how much a reality widowhood is for the middle-aged:

PERCENTAGES OF PERSONS WIDOWED IN VARIOUS AGE GROUPS
(Based on total population of persons 18 and over)

Age	Males	Females
35–44	0.5%	2.9%
45–54	1.4%	8.2%
55–64	3.5%	20.6%

That last figure cannot be ignored: one fifth of all American women between the ages of 55 and 64 are widows.

It is to be hoped, of course, that with proper attention to diet and exercise, and with further advances in medical research and practice, the figure will decrease. But until and unless it changes dramatically, the best word we have for women in mid-life is that you may well be widowed, that it will be terrible beyond belief if it happens—but that you can not only survive it, you can be genuinely happy again. In a general way, you will be helped by all of the factors that have improved so many facets of middle-aged life: the economic outlook, the social and professional opportunities, and the more permissive and liberated *Zeitgeist* all make widowhood far less dreadful than it was a generation ago. But part of your success in dealing with widowhood, if you are called upon to do so, will depend on your willingness to face the possibility now, and to be prepared for it.

Do you find it too grisly even to think about the possibility of being widowed? The numbers are still there, and your failure to face them won't change them. Nor will facing them squarely hasten your husband's death. Honestly. The chances are four to one that you will *not* be a widow before you are 65, but *just in case*, a little preparation now will help you to get through the crisis period—and do much more than that, afterward.

What makes a "successful" widow—one who eventually picks up the pieces of her life and makes it whole and good again—and what makes an "unsuccessful" widow—one who spends the rest of her days in mourning, depression, anger, or helpless dependence on others? The answer is complex, perhaps not even fully known, but fortunately, a few of the well-understood points are as elementary as they are important. And since widowers, though there are far fewer of them, are not insignificant in number, it is worth noting that many of these points apply to them as well as to widows.

The outstanding prerequisite for good recovery after the death of a spouse is a strong ego structure, a sense of respect for one's own identity. The woman who has never thought of herself as anything but a wife is almost surely doomed, for when she isn't a wife any more, she has, by her own standard, ceased to exist. On the other hand, the wife who also sees herself as a career woman, a board member of a club, a force in the community, a significant person to a large circle of friends, a reader, a concert-goer, art lover, collector of stamps or butterflies, gardener, choir singer, horsewoman, cellist, swimmer, pot-maker, rug-weaver, conservationist, political party worker—anything at all, no matter what—will continue to be *something*, not just a nonwife, which is nothing. Women who function on a variety of levels, if they are ever widowed, have an immense advantage over those who do not; extra hours spent with the garden club or on the tennis-tournament committee cannot make up for the absence of a mate—but they are certainly a big improvement over hours spent alone with nothing to do, week after week and year after year.

A recent book on widowhood has been well reviewed, which puzzles us, for we agree with little that it has to say. For one thing, the author states that most women find their identity through their husbands and sink to the lowest step of the ranking order without them. The crucial—and dead-wrong—word here is *most*. Today, thanks to the influence of the women's liberation movement, *most* women find their identities, at least in large part, through themselves—through their own ideas, creativity, work, accomplishments, relationships with others. Most women are what they think and do, and are not merely extensions of someone else, becoming nonpersons when that someone dies.

There are still a minority who fall into the old-fashioned Adam's rib category, however, and they have serious work to do. The first step in creating an independent identity is to realize that, if necessary, you could at least deal with the physical necessities of daily life, even though your emotional problems might be close to overwhelming. We hasten to add that this does not apply to the first days or weeks after bereavement, but to the time after that. We have met, listened to, heard about, and read about widows who wailed (a little boastfully, perhaps?) that they had never learned to write a check, pay a bill, unplug the toilet, change a fuse, or even *hire* someone to trim the hedge or cut the grass. Any woman who can't do all of those things by the time she is middle-aged is sadly deficient in normal skills. And any woman who, like the author of the book we alluded to, moves out of the city and into the suburbs without knowing how to drive a car (and turns out to be unable to learn) must be a total fool. But of course there are some women— like Jennifer W., whom we met in Chapter 6—who only grow older but never more mature; they make their way through life being helpless little girls and letting others take care of them and solve their problems. Psychiatrists' offices are filled with them, for if such women are widowed, they soon find—as did the widow-author —that the friends on whom they depend too much, for much too long, must eventually extricate themselves and go back to their own lives; even the best friends in the world cannot indefinitely be caretakers, as was the late indulgent daddy-husband.

Occasionally, one is astonished by an apparently helpless wife who turns out to be nothing of the sort. Lillian P., an old friend who belongs to the generation before ours, is a case in point. Her husband, Martin, used to make jokes about the fact that she had never learned to drive (a good thing, he said, because she was so unmechanical that she would probably wreck the car within a week), she couldn't use a checkbook (her simple arithmetic was so simple as to be useless), she couldn't hang a picture (she didn't know the difference between a hammer and a screwdriver), she couldn't be trusted to make any decision more complicated than choosing what to serve for dinner (she was a whimsical and unclear thinker). When Martin died, everyone feared for Lillian; her dependence on him had been so absolute that her survival without him seemed questionable. Friends milled around for a while, but then, rather suddenly, Lillian was no longer available for visits and was even hard to reach on the telephone. We all called each other and worried.

After some months, Lillian told her secret: she had enrolled in a driving course, gotten her license, and was so enchanted with her new accomplishment that she went driving off into the country nearly every day, both for practice and for the pure heady pleasure of it. Relieved of the burden of preparing elaborate meals and keeping house for an unusually demanding husband, she had also joined a national women's organization and was participating in every program offered. Within the year, Lillian became the president of her local chapter. At about the same time, she began to travel extensively, and as she proved to be a gifted public speaker, she eventually registered with a lecture bureau and toured the country, giving travel lectures to other women's clubs.

At this juncture it finally dawned on all of us that Lillian had never been a helpless wife at all, but had only pretended to be one. She had been the victim of a domineering and insecure husband who *needed* a helpless wife, and to keep the peace Lillian had played the game. (As we said, she belongs to an older generation than ours.) But freed from bondage, she became a different person—the real Lillian. She has been a widow for many years now, and although never interested in another marriage (who can blame her?), she is eminently alive, eager, brimming with excitement, and forever rushing from one interesting event to another. She might (or might not) be shocked to hear us say this, but she seems to be much happier as a widow than she ever was as a wife.

Lillian is not typical, though, for it is almost always the happier wives who make a good adjustment to widowhood. When an endlessly mourning widow tells you, "I loved him so much, he was my whole life; I can *never* take any interest in anything or anybody without him," you are entitled to doubts. Such an attitude is perfectly normal for a while, but if it persists for several years, there is more at work than normal grief. As Sigmund Freud said of mourning in *Mourning and Melancholia,* "We rely on its being overcome after a certain lapse of time, and we look upon any interference with it as useless or even harmful. . . . [But] when the work of mourning is completed the ego becomes free and uninhibited again."

The bereaved widow who talks forever about the glories of her dead marriage may actually have had a miserable marriage, and may feel guilty about her relief at being rid of her husband. It is typical of such persons that they spend the rest of their years convincing themselves, and all who will listen, that the dreadful union was idyllic. (We couldn't help wondering as we read our unfavorite book about widowhood if the author would have been less "crazy," as she puts it, for so long, if she had found a little time to look in on her dying husband during his last thirteen days of life.)

Another reason for prolonged grief may be a failure ever to have resolved the anxiety we all feel, as children, when we are separated from our mothers. This is a common cause of insecurity in adults, and when a husband or wife dies, the sudden abandonment can elicit a lasting depression that stems from childhood fears and is out of proportion to the more recent event. In addition, the survivor is often angry with the deceased for having abandoned him or her and, failing to understand the psychodynamics of that anger, feels guilty about it; as a result, the anger is repressed and takes the substitute form of depression. The only way we know to deal with such problems is to work them out in psychotherapy; they don't go away by themselves.

On a simpler but highly practical level, financial problems are often a cause of continuing depression, too. There is nothing neurotic about being depressed if you can't pay the rent—but it may be neurotic, or at least poor judgment, to wait until rent day comes around to find out what the financial score is. Do you know what your assets and income would be if your husband died tomorrow? Can you maintain your present living arrangements on your own income? Can you maintain *any* acceptable living arrangements on that income? Will you get insurance money? If so, how much? Are you entitled to any portion of your husband's retirement or pension fund at this time? If so, what portion and how much does it come to? What about Social Security—what are you eligible for, if anything? (You can pick up a booklet that explains Social Security benefits at your local Social Security office or at the post office.) Do you know where all the bank books are? The safe deposit box? Are you a co-signer for it and do you have a key? (When the bank learns of a death it seals the box; if you are prepared, you are there first.) Do you have a list of all insurance policies and do you know where they are? What about securities, real-estate deeds, debts payable? If there is anything you are not fully informed about, get to work. If you never have need of the information, you won't have lost anything by acquiring it; if you do need it, it will make all the difference between suffering enormous grief and suffering enormous grief together with enormous economic panic.

It is not ghoulish to know in advance what you would have to do in order to live if your husband were to die; you have every right to know. Would he be upset if you asked him for complete financial information? Too bad. Do it anyway, because it is infinitely better for him to be upset now, and for the two of you to play out the scene together, than for you to have to do it all alone at a time when you are ill equipped to do anything. Except resent his leaving you unprepared.

Donald I. Rogers wrote a book with the excellent and unforgettable title *Teach Your Wife to Be a Widow.* Men *should* teach their wives to be widows—if they need to; we would prefer to think that at this stage of social evolution, women are able and willing to teach themselves. It goes without saying, of course, that husbands should learn about their wives' financial affairs, too, in case they become widowers. With a large proportion of wives working, women's insurance policies, pension plans, bank accounts, stock accounts, and so forth are no longer rare as they once were. It is bound to be helpful to a recently bereaved husband if he doesn't have to tear the house apart, or go on a treasure hunt, to find all of the carefully put away documents. It's helpful, too, if he knows how to prepare a simple meal and run the washing machine—but then, we like to think that most men do these days.

Since we're playing the law of averages, we must return to women once more. Let's assume that you have read all of the preceding with care and have decided that you are definitely your own person and have no problems with your identity; you've rattled all the skeletons in the closet and concluded that you have been a pretty good wife and have nothing to feel guilty about; you are well in touch with the financial picture and know exactly what kind of life-style you could manage if you were widowed. Will all that make it easy for you if it happens? No, it won't. Nothing will. But it will help you to get over the crisis, to stop being just a widow, and to start being a full-fledged happy person again. Like many a divorced person, a newly bereaved spouse feels that life has ended, and for the moment it has. But in time, when all the grief work—the uninhibited mourning, with an exploration and understanding of its many complicated aspects—has been done, then, and only then, can the mourner return fully to life. Progress is made a step at a time; as the work of mourning gets done, reentry into the everyday world becomes possible, and when mourning comes to an end, reentry is complete. For one who is in the time of deepest despair, it is impossible to believe that life can ever be good again. But it *can*. We say so with absolute confidence because we ourselves have found it to be true.

Bernice comments

David was a psychoanalyst. He was also a bright, perceptive, engaging, wise, and very funny man. We had a fine marriage and looked forward to many, many more years of it.

One Friday afternoon, I went along while David had his annual medical checkup, since we were planning to drive out to the country right from the doctor's office. After a long whispered conference in the laboratory technician's office, the doctor contrived to see me alone for just a moment while David was dressing. Avoiding my eyes, he said hastily, "The red count is low and I thought I saw a few funny-looking cells on the blood slide; nothing definite, really; don't say anything about it, I'll call."

We drove off to the country, David in high spirits, I with cold fear in my stomach and the taste of panic in my mouth, trying desperately to sound normal. I didn't have to play-act for very long. The doctor phoned David the next morning and came straight to the point: he had shown the blood slide to a pathologist and they both thought the white cells looked leukemic. Definitive tests could only be done in the hospital.

We simply walked out of the house and into the car. (Many weeks later I would remember to ask friends to go and scrape the moldy food out of the refrigerator.) We drove directly to the hospital, where David was admitted at once. The next day a bone-marrow biopsy confirmed the worst possible suspicion: he had acute myelogenous leukemia. A fatal disease, we were told, that might run its course in as little as two weeks—but there was a new and highly sophisticated treatment, a possibility of a remission . . . of course, yes, we would try it, even if the chance was a very small one. David, in two days, was already running a fever and beginning to feel weak. He died two months later.

I don't want to dwell on those two months except to pass on information which might be useful to others. First, we both knew that chances of a remission were slim and we wanted very much to be together for whatever time remained. Because we had excellent medical insurance that covered most of the (astronomical) bills, and because The New York Hospital had a huge private room with a sofa in it, I was able to move in and stay for the duration. Such a plan might not suit everyone's needs, but it was of immeasurable help to us. For although the hospital staff was splendid, they had many patients to care for while I had only one; I could keep the I.V.'s from dripping too fast or too slowly, watch to see that they didn't clog or infuse; when the chills and searing fevers came, I could pile on the four extra blankets or give an alcohol sponge faster than any nurse could even answer the light. I was there to make sure that no one gave him a forbidden aspirin by mistake or failed to notice the big red ALLERGIC TO PENICILLIN warning on the chart. I was able to fulfill the important function of screening visitors on bad days, monitoring phone calls, even turning away eager young interns come to perform torturous medical procedures at times when they simply could not be borne. Would David have died any sooner had I not been there? Maybe not, but he was certainly more comfortable—and so was I—because I *was* there.

And in the middle of all that was happening, we had a kind of sad and beautiful life together. The local liquor store sent up cold white wine at dinner hour every night; we never ate the dinner but we did enjoy the wine. Somehow, we found things to laugh about, and often we wept for ourselves and each other, overcome by the terrible thing that was happening, but still hoping that it would go away. It was a poignantly intimate and very special time for us, painful and precious in equal measure. I am deeply grateful for those weeks. I don't know if living-in arrangements can commonly be made in hospitals, but for anyone who wants to do it, it's worth a try; hospital administrators are just as human as other people, and if they can help, they will.

The biggest source of outside strength throughout the hospital period was people. First, my children, who had suddenly, and for the first time, assumed parental roles. My daughter Barbara, who lived in Manhattan, came every day with a Styrofoam ice bucket filled with delicious hot food. I couldn't eat anything—but of course I had to, because she had gone to so much trouble. Emaciated as I quickly became anyway, I think I would have collapsed altogether without her care. And all of the children came to sit and chat, to bring gossip and news of the outside world, to fill the room with cheer and love. And so did scores of friends. Sometimes, when I sneaked out to the nurses' cafeteria for a few minutes in the middle of the night for coffee, I would find a friend or two sitting on the floor in the hall-way—*just sitting there*—in case I came out and wanted to talk. In times of crisis, the people who love you are more valuable than anything else in the world. *It helps to know that when you are in deep trouble, others can sustain you.*

There was even help from people I didn't know. Each day, stacks of donor slips arrived from the blood bank. Perhaps half of them were from friends, but the others bore strange names, the friends of friends.

Mixed among the many supportive and dear friends there were also a few well-meaning undesirables; these were the weepers who arrived with tears already flowing and the sobs still held in check but obviously all ready to go. At first, David could turn on his best therapeutic manner and have them laughing within seconds. When he grew too ill to make that effort, and I too weary, I simply refused to let them into the room. Their feelings were undoubtedly hurt and we were sorry for that, but we couldn't take the wear and tear they engendered. *Don't use your energy to cheer up outsiders.* This is the one time—perhaps the only time—when it is all right to take more than you give.

Very suddenly, it seemed, the drama drew to an abrupt close. One morning at five o'clock I knew it was the last day. I went out to a phone booth in the hall and within minutes, it seemed, the children and a few dear friends were there. David fell into a coma, doctors and nurses with a battalion of machines took over the room, and I sat with my little group in the solarium. We sat all day, tense, stiff, silent. In the late afternoon the doctor came and motioned me to return to the room. David was dead. I couldn't believe it. No matter what you know intellectually, there is no way to be prepared emotionally for the death of someone you love. It comes with the suddenness of lightning, the force of a tidal wave.

I was allowed a few minutes alone to say my goodbyes, and then the doctor came for me again. I was immediately ushered into a small crowded room and bombarded with questions and forms to sign. I was conscious that people were asking me insane questions about "disposition of the body," funeral directors, clergymen, autopsy permissions, would I like personally to write the obituary notice for *The New York Times*? Peculiar as it seems, I believe I answered all those questions; I must have, since everything got done just the way I wanted it.

How did I know what I wanted? A few years before, David and I had talked about that faraway time when one of us might die, and pondered what we would do. Neither of us was religious, we both favored cremation, donation of all possible parts to science, and I went on record as being opposed to funerals. Somehow, the funeral question was left hanging, but during the hospital period, David, a psychologist to the end, asked me what I planned to do about a funeral "in case" he died. "Nothing," I said, "unless you want something." "It won't make any difference to me," David answered, "but it will to you and the children and all of our friends. People who have been involved need a chance to say goodbye, and there is strength and solidarity in doing it together. A death without some kind of group ritual is like a sentence without a period, a melody without a resolution—it just trails off, but it never really ends."

What wise words those were. I must have given them some thought, consciously or not, because sitting there dazed in that packed, airless room, within five minutes I made all the plans for a service and asked that several of David's close friends be called and asked to speak. One of them was Morton.

When I emerged into the hallway, my son Eugene was waiting with a wheelchair piled high with all of the possessions that had accumulated in two months of hospital living. There were the clothes that David had worn when he was admitted, my suitcase, gifts, books, a radio, his list of patients with their addresses and phone numbers which he had never left out of his sight. It was a Kafkaesque kind of moving day, the end of an era, the end of a life, a life all heaped in a wheelchair. It was one week before David's 50th birthday.

After that was a blur. The apartment full of people, I full of numb despair, still not sure it was real. Friends flowed in and out, meals got cooked and served, someone kept giving me pills. I remember almost nothing of it except the dumb agony. My only clear recollection of that first night is that I sat down at my desk (as I had promised David I would) and clearly and lucidly wrote a note, by hand, to every one of his patients. I told them what had happened and gave them the name of another therapist they could contact if they wanted to talk about it. They all did.

The funeral was a blur, too. I sat in the front row and never looked back. I was told that there were hundreds of people but I never saw them. I was focused on my three children, my two sons-in-law, the people on whom my very life depended at that time. I also listened intently to the speakers and actually heard everything they said. I can still remember some of it. For the first time I heard myself referred to as a "widow," an exotic and horrid word. It would be some time before I could utter it with ease.

When the service was over, I left through a small private door that opened onto a side street. About two weeks later I had an idea that as my son was leading me to the car, I had seen my former analyst standing there waiting for me. He said, "As soon as you are able, I want you to call me." I wasn't even positive that it had really happened, but I called him anyway. Avrum, bless you.

Then it really began. The hordes of visitors started to trail off. I started to insist that the children stop taking turns sleeping at my apartment and resume their normal lives; the first night that I was alone is one I will never, ever forget, but once I had done it I knew that I could.

Friends stayed in close touch, I was never alone for dinner, and above all, I had my therapy sessions to cling to twice a week. The first thing I learned from them was a genuine revelation to me, something that contradicted my belief of a lifetime: *I didn't have to be a heroine, I didn't even have to be a little bit brave.* It was perfectly all right to cry whenever I needed to (most of the time), to talk about David obsessively, to let my friends befriend me without feeling guilty or embarrassed, because they *wanted* to help. If I prevented them, my therapist said, it would not only hurt me, but would hurt them as well because I would be rejecting their friendship. What a useful piece of knowledge that was. I accepted every dinner invitation that came my way and blubbered at some of the loveliest tables in town. And in a while I began to feel better.

This experience is not unique but is well supported by a great deal of psychological literature. David Maddison of the University of Sydney studied conjugal bereavement in 132 young and middle-aged women and reported his findings in the *British Journal of Medical Psychology* in September 1968. He said that widows with a poor outcome felt that they lacked permissive environmental support and that their expressions of affect (feeling, emotion) had been blocked. Dr. Francis J. Braceland, an editor of *The Year Book of Psychiatry and Applied Mental Health (1970)*, added this footnote to Dr. Maddison's paper:

> It is recognized now that one who is bereaved and has lost a loved one must mourn. It is only when mourning lasts too long and the widow's weeds become a custom for years that one begins to wonder about the depression. . . .
>
> Dr. Maddison's article has several facets. Widows rated as having a bad outcome after bereavement reported a high frequency of unhelpful interviews with persons in their social

network in the three months after the husband's death. These individuals should be worked with [by a therapist] during the crisis itself and during the period of mourning if they request it. Admonition to keep a stiff upper lip and control oneself is fatuous and harmful. They are in need of a kind, understanding listener who stands by as they work out and express their grief.

While the above was intended for professional therapists, the role of kind, understanding listener is played for the great majority of people by their friends. They may, indeed, be just as effective as professionals if they will actually stand by while the widow works out and expresses her grief—and *if the widow allows them to play that role.*

The proof for me that I was returning to life was that as the tears began to taper off, I began to work. Not much, at first, but I did get some words down on paper and I knew that I was pointed in the right direction.

There were still days that were hideous, the *special* days—birthdays, anniversaries, Thanksgiving, Christmas, and so forth. Friends who had been through it said, "The first year is the hardest. Once you have passed each milestone, it's easier the second time around." It was true.

When spring came, I suddenly needed to go back to the country house I had left in haste and terror. It was one more milestone that I had to pass and my son went with me to help. All of David's things were where he had left them, and I cried all day. But then we began to clean up the mess in the garden and the sight of green was good and the symbol of new life was welcome and reassuring.

The country was especially precious that year because I thought I might not be back again; it was clear that I could not afford both the country house and the city apartment, and in a while, one or the other—probably the house—would have to go. But not yet. I had enough money to live on for a while, even allowing for my meager work output that season. The only decision I made turned out to be one of the best I have ever made, and I recommend it without reservation: I would make no other decisions until a year had passed. I still had some time, and though I was beginning to *feel* compos mentis, I wasn't quite sure I could trust my judgment enough to sell houses or apartments.

But before my year was up, Morton came to tell me that his marriage had fallen apart. It had been happening, but, immersed as I was in my own troubles, I hadn't known anything about it. I was so distressed by the sad news that I wept. Then we talked about David and we both wept. We shared a lot of sympathy, empathy, friendship, and dinners in those next weeks. Morton helped turn over the garden so that I could get the tomatoes in on time. By the time the crop was ready for harvest, we knew that we loved each other, Morton's divorce had gone through, and it seemed only natural for us to get married at once.

Had I forgotten about David? No, not then, not now, not ever. I think of him often, I talk about him often, and I still marvel at how much he taught me. But I talk about him without sadness, without pain, without mourning. It is a long time since I stopped thinking or dreaming about the nightmare scenes in the hospital, but I still remember most of the happy times we shared. Morton and I frequently recollect some of the funny things David used to say and do and we chuckle over them with pleasure. We even like to speculate about how very pleased David would be if he could know how happy we are together.

Do I love Morton more or less than I loved David? That question has no answer. I love him *differently*. He's a different person from David and, moreover, I'm a different person from the one I used to be. I don't think that anyone can go through the experience of widowhood without profound change. I have a different perspective about life, a different sense of values. I learned that it is important to do the things we really want to do and not put them off for some future time, for every second is precious and should be enjoyed to the fullest. I learned that most of the things we get upset about are trivial and not worth the energy we pour into them or the discomfort we cause others; I learned that material items are of no value whatsoever for none is irreplaceable, and the only things that are of monumental importance are life and love.

Even if I hadn't changed within myself, I couldn't possibly have related to Morton the same way I did to David because the interac-

tion between oneself and any other individuals is always different. I
don't try to compare the marriages because they are too unlike to be
compared. They are alike only in that my life is full and complete and
I am as happy as I ever was or could be.

While a new marriage was the best of all outcomes for me, it was
not the only one possible. By the time I remarried, it was clear that I
could have made a go of single life and been, though not nearly as
happy as I am now, a successful widow nonetheless, as Lillian and
many other widows are and for the same reasons. I did not die with
David; I did my mourning and when it was over, I still had myself, my
work, my friends, my family, my interests, my pleasures. I never felt
that to enjoy myself without David was in any way disloyal. In fact, he
would have been appalled if I *hadn't* enjoyed myself. One of the
things that made him so well loved by so many people was his
enormous zest for life, for making the most of every moment. It was
evident in everything he said and did, which made him a most remarkable teacher. He taught his friends and patients alike, by word
and by example, never to close one's eyes to beauty, to actively
pursue happiness, to look for humor and joy in every situation, and
always search within and be true to one's own feelings. I think he
would be well pleased with me.

Morton comments

I still recall the gray, broken, lifeless look of Bernice's face when,
immediately after David's funeral, I and a number of others joined
her at her apartment. Yet even then, in that dreadful hour, it came to
me in a flash of insight that she was the kind of person who would
slowly climb back up out of the abyss, and would someday love
again, and greatly. What gave me that sudden insight was my recognition of the similarity between Bernice and another widow I had
known.

Her name was Rose, and for a few years in the later part of her life
she was my stepmother. Prior to that, Rose had had a long and happy
marriage, and when she was widowed at 59, it never occurred to any
of her friends and relatives that she would ever marry again. After all,
she was far from young, she was a self-sufficient businesswoman, she
had a large number of nieces and nephews to whom she was devoted

(she had had no children of her own); and above all, she had loved her husband very much, and he her.

But what her friends and relatives did not realize was that a woman or man who has had a deep, rewarding love relationship is less likely to remain frozen in the widowed state than one whose marriage was mediocre or even poor. For the person who has been accustomed for many years to the giving and receiving of love, to being a second self to another and having that other be one's own second self, has an imperious need to love again, to be complete again. That need propels such a person, with great force, toward a new relationship.

For people like Rose, a new love is no admission of disloyalty to the old, but an affirmation that the lost love was too good not to be replaced. Two years after her husband died, Rose married my father (who had been widowed three years before). They loved each other dearly and with almost youthful wonder, and were thoroughly happy together for five years. Then my father died, and Rose, in her late 60's, was a widow for the second time. Again she suffered, recovered, and made a busy and successful life for herself in her widowhood. Who could have imagined—but need I go on? At 71, Rose—still full of love and still hungering for love, still pledging allegiance to life—married a retired building contractor and had four years of warm affectionate married life with him. And then he, too, died, and Rose, in her mid-70's, was a widow for the third time.

That should be the end of the story, but it isn't, quite. For I still recall a day, seven years later, when we met at Thanksgiving dinner and Rose, nearing 82, and in failing health, told me proudly and with a twinkle in her eye about the "gentleman friend" she had recently met, and of whom she was becoming very fond, as he was of her. Only a few weeks later she died rather suddenly, but I have little doubt that had she lived, she would once more, optimistically and excitedly, have entered into another marriage.

All this came to my mind that afternoon when we had gathered in Bernice's apartment to give her such poor comfort as we could. As soon as it occurred to me, and without even considering whether it was a proper or improper thing to do, I drew Bernice apart and said to her, as nearly as I can recall, "I know you won't believe what I'm going to tell you, but I feel certain that you will not only make your way back to life, but that someday you will love again," and I told her, briefly, about Rose. She looked at me blankly, as if she had hardly heard or understood what I had said, but squeezed my hand in a gesture of appreciation.

Half a year later, Bernice was beginning to function again more or less normally, and it was just then that those events in my own life of which we have spoken earlier threw us together. My prediction about her came true—and miraculously, unexpectedly, it was she and I, together, who made it so. But everything she has written about herself above, and everything I have just said, make me certain that had it not been I, it would eventually have been another. How extraordinary that by a sheer accident of timing, it was not another, but I. For it is with her, and through her, that I have been able, after the defeat of a second divorce, to experience my middle age as the Prime Time of my life; and, she tells me, it is with me, and through me, after the pain of being widowed that the same thing has become possible for her.

Source Notes

Major works named in the text and listed in the bibliography are not duplicated here. Works referred to here by author's last name only are cited in full in the bibliography.

CHAPTER 1

The decline in median age at birth of last child between 1890 and 1950: Paul C. Glick, "The Family Cycle," *American Sociological Review*, vol. 12 (1947), and Glick, *American Families*. New York: Wiley, 1957.

Present-day median age of mother at birth of last child: Arthur J. Norton, "The Family Life-cycle Updated: Components and Uses." In Winch and Spanier, 1974. The figures we have given are for white women; those for black women are a little higher.

There is no middle-age crisis: John A. Clausen, in Riley, vol. 3, 1972.

Many older people describe their middle years as happiest: Leland J. Axelson, in Vedder, 1965, and John A. Clausen, in Riley, vol. 3, 1972.

Place of older people in primitive societies: Leo W. Simmons, "Attitudes Toward Aging and Aged: Primitive Societies." *Journal of Gerontology*, vol. 1 (1946).

CHAPTER 2

Leland J. Axelson: in Vedder, 1965.

Dr. Leslie S. Libow, *Human Aging II: An Eleven-Year Followup Biomedical and Behavioral Study*. DHEW pub. no. (HSM) 71-9037.

Dr. K. Warner Schaie: Baltes and Schaie, "The Myth of the Twilight Years," *Psychology Today*, March 1974.

Queens College adult-education program: *New York Times*, May 9, 1973.

CHAPTER 3

Duration of marriages ending in divorce: *Vital Statistics of the United States, 1969,* vol. 3: Marriage and Divorce, tables 2-5, 2-6.

Husbands rarely talked to their wives: Robert S. Lynd and Helen M. Lynd, *Middletown: A Study in Contemporary American Culture.* New York: Harcourt, 1929.

David L. Cohn, *Love in America: An Informal Study of Manners and Morals in American Marriage.* New York: Simon and Schuster, 1943.

CHAPTER 4

Brandeis University sentence-completion test: P. Golde and N. Kogan, "A Sentence Completion Procedure for Assessing Attitudes Toward Old People." *Journal of Gerontology,* vol. 14 (July 1959).

Duke University study: Gustave Newman and Claude R. Nichols, in De Martino, 1966.

Two interview excerpts beginning "I love my sex," and "[After some years of marriage]": previously published in part in Hunt, 1974.

Diabetic men and impotence: A. Rubin and D. Babbott, "Impotence and Diabetes Mellitus," *Journal of the American Medical Association,* vol. 168 (October 4, 1968).

Herman Hellerstein and Ernest Friedman, "Sexual Activity and the Post-coronary Patient," *Medical Aspects of Human Sexuality,* March 1969.

Helen Kaplan and Clifford Sager, "Sexual Patterns at Different Ages," *Medical Aspects of Human Sexuality,* June 1971.

CHAPTER 5

"The Awareness of Middle Age," in Neugarten, 1968.

Safety records of older workers: Governor's Commission on the Employment and Retirement Problems of Older Workers, *Employment and Retirement of Older Workers.* Sacramento: State Printing Office, 1960.

Absenteeism of older workers: David Dressler, *Sociology: The Study of Human Interaction.* New York: Knopf, 1969.

Dr. Wayne Dennis: "Creative Productivity Between the Ages of 20 and 80 Years," adapted from *Journal of Gerontology,* vol. 21, no. 1 (January 1966).

Robert F. Peck: in Neugarten, 1968.

Possible results of extramarital relationships—a short reading list:

Hunt, Morton, *The Affair.* New York: World, 1969.

Libby, Roger W., and Whitehurst, Robert N. (eds.), *Renovating Marriage: Toward New Sexual Life-styles.* Danville: Consensus, 1973.

Neubeck, Gerhard (ed.), *Extramarital Relations.* Englewood Cliffs: Prentice-Hall, 1969. Paper.

O'Neill, Nena, and O'Neill, George, *Open Marriage.* New York: Evans, 1972.

Rogers, Carl R. *Becoming Partners: Marriage and Its Alternatives.* New York: Delacorte, 1972.

Success ratio of marriage counseling: Beck, Dorothy Fahs, and Jones, Mary Ann, *Progress on Family Problems: A Nationwide Study of Clients' and Counselors' Views on Family Agency Services.* New York: Family Service Association of America, Inc., 1973.

CHAPTER 6

Professor Neugarten: in Neugarten, 1968.

Pension reform act: *New York Times,* September 3, 1974.

John L. Thomas, "Marital Failure and Duration," *Social Order,* vol. 3 (January 1953).

John A. Clausen: in Riley, vol. 3, 1972.

Harris Schrank: in Riley, vol. 3, 1972.

CHAPTER 7

Dr. William E. Connor: *New York Times,* November 29, 1973, and personal communication from Dr. Connor.

Dr. Peter Frommer: *Medical World News,* April 19, 1974.

Dr. Hollis S. Ingraham: ibid.

Finnish heart study: *New York Times,* September 16, 1973.

Low-cholesterol diet protects against some forms of cancer: *New York Times,* March 26, 1974.

Robert Half: *New York Times,* January 2, 1974.

Dr. William Nolen: *McCall's,* August 1973.

Sex-therapy clinics: *New York Times,* May 5, 1974, and *Medical World News,* May 10, 1974.

A list of Masters and Johnson-trained therapists:

Dorothy and Armando DeMoya, Washington, D.C.

Alexandra Fauntleroy and John Reckless, Duke University, Durham, North Carolina.

Virginia Lozzi and Alexander N. Levay, New York City.

Audrey and Harvey Resnik, Chevy Chase, Maryland.

Lorna and Philip M. Sarrel, Yale Department of Student Health, New Haven, Connecticut.

Marguerite and Marshall Shearer, Ann Arbor, Michigan.

Joanne and Philip Veenhuis, Wauwatosa, Wisconsin.

Dr. Arlie Russell Hochschild: *Society,* July/August 1973.

Nursing homes: see Jacoby, Mendelson; *New York Times,* October 7, 8, 9, 10, 1974.

Low-cholesterol cookbooks: see American Heart Association, Revell, Rosenthal, Zugibe.

CHAPTER 8

Dr. Paul Gebhard: in Bohannan, 1971.

Suicide rates: *Mortality from Selected Causes by Marital Status.* DHEW, Vital and Health Statistics, series 20, no. 8a, Part A.

Protective nature of marriage: Walter R. Gove, "Sex, Marital Status, and Mortality," *American Journal of Sociology,* July 1973.

Dr. Alex Comfort: *Single,* August 1973.

Remarriage of divorced persons of all ages: *Current Population Reports,* series P-20, no. 239, "Marriage, Divorce, and Remarriage by Year of Birth, June 1971," Bureau of the Census. Remarriage of persons divorcing between 40 and 45: direct communication from Arthur J. Norton, chief of Marriage and Family Statistics Branch, Bureau of the Census.

Psychiatric outpatient admissions: Michael J. Witkin, *Outpatient Psychiatric Services, 1971–72.* NIMH series A, no. 13. Rockville: DHEW, 1974.

Bibliography

The American Heart Association. *The American Heart Association Cookbook*. New York: McKay, 1973.

Barnard, Christiaan. *Heart Attack: You Don't Have to Die*. New York: Dell, 1973. Paper.

Bergler, Edmund. *Divorce Won't Help*. New York: Harper, 1948.

Bernard, Jessie. *Remarriage: A Study of Marriage*. New York: Dryden, 1956.

———. *The Future of Marriage*. New York: World, 1972.

———. *The Sex Game*. New York: Atheneum, 1972. Paper.

Blood, Robert O., Jr., and Wolfe, Donald M. *Husbands and Wives: The Dynamics of Married Living*. Chicago: Free Press, 1960.

Bohannan, Paul (ed.). *Divorce and After*. Garden City: Doubleday Anchor, 1971. Paper.

Boston Women's Health Book Collective. *Our Bodies, Ourselves: A Book By and For Women*. New York: Simon and Schuster, 1973. Paper.

Bullough, Vern L., and Bullough, Bonnie. *The Subordinate Sex: A History of Attitudes Toward Women*. Urbana: University of Illinois Press, 1973.

Comfort, Alex (ed.). *The Joy of Sex: A Gourmet Guide to Lovemaking*. New York: Crown, 1972.

Cuber, John F., and Harroff, Peggy B. *The Significant Americans*. New York: Appleton-Century, 1965.

Curtin, Sharon R. *Nobody Ever Died of Old Age*. Boston: Little, Brown, 1972.

de Beauvoir, Simone. *The Coming of Age*. New York: Putnam, 1972.

De Martino, Manfred F. (ed.). *Sexual Behavior and Personality Characteristics*. New York: Grove Press, 1966. Paper.

Dennis, Wayne. "Creative Productivity Between the Ages of 20 and 80 Years," *Journal of Gerontology*, vol. 21, no. 1 (January 1966).

Dolger, Henry, and Seeman, Bernard. *How to Live with Diabetes*. New York: Pyramid, 1966. Paper.

Erikson, Erik H. *Childhood and Society*. 2nd ed. New York: Norton, 1963.

———. *Insight and Responsibility*. New York: Norton, 1964.

Freud, Sigmund. *The Standard Edition of the Complete Psychological Works of Sigmund Freud.* London: Hogarth Press, 1959.

Gertler, Menard M. *You Can Predict Your Heart Attack and Prevent It.* New York: Random House, 1963.

Glick, Paul C., and Norton, Arthur J. "Perspectives on the Recent Upturn in Divorce and Remarriage." Bureau of the Census, Social and Economics Statistics Administration, U.S. Department of Commerce. Mimeographed edition of paper delivered in Toronto, April 13–15, 1972.

Goffman, Erving. *Relations in Public: Microstudies of the Public Order.* New York: Basic Books, 1971.

Goode, William J. *After Divorce.* Glencoe: Free Press, 1956.

Gould, Roger L. "The Phases of Adult Life: A Study in Developmental Psychology," *American Journal of Psychiatry,* vol. 129:5 (November 1972).

Hunt, Morton. *The Natural History of Love.* New York: Knopf, 1959.

——. *Her Infinite Variety: The American Woman as Lover, Mate and Rival.* New York: Harper and Row, 1962.

——. *The World of the Formerly Married.* New York: McGraw-Hill, 1966.

——. *The Affair: A Portrait of Extra-Marital Love in Contemporary America.* New York: World, 1969.

——. *Sexual Behavior in the 1970s.* New York: Playboy Press, 1974.

Jacoby, Susan. "Waiting for the End: On Nursing Homes," *New York Times Magazine,* March 31, 1974.

Kinsey, Alfred; Pomeroy, Wardell B.; and Martin, Clyde E. *Sexual Behavior in the Human Male.* Philadelphia: Saunders, 1948.

——, and Gebhard, Paul H. *Sexual Behavior in the Human Female.* Philadelphia: Saunders, 1953.

Lindbergh, Anne Morrow. *Gift from the Sea.* New York: Vintage, 1955. Paper.

Masters, William H., and Johnson, Virginia E. *Human Sexual Response.* Boston: Little, Brown, 1966.

——. *Human Sexual Inadequacy.* Boston: Little, Brown, 1970.

Mendelson, Mary Adelaide. *Tender Loving Greed.* New York: Knopf, 1974.

Menopause and Aging. See Ryan and Gibson.

Metropolitan Life Statistical Bulletin, vol. 44 (September 1963): "The Prevalence of Chronic Conditions."

——, vol. 51 (July 1970): "Diabetes at Midlife."

Morris, James R. *Employment Opportunities in Later Years.* Burlingame: Foundation for Voluntary Welfare, 1960.

Neugarten, Bernice L. (ed.). *Middle Age and Aging: A Reader in Social Psychology.* Chicago: University of Chicago Press, 1968.

———, and associates. *Personality in Middle and Late Life*. New York: Atherton, 1964.

Peterson, James Alfred. *Married Love in the Middle Years*. New York: Association Press, 1968.

Reiss, Ira L. *Hetero-Sexual Relationships: Inside and Outside of Marriage*. Morristown: General Learning Press, 1973.

Revell, Dorothy. *Cholesterol Control Cookery*. Berkeley: Berkeley Medallion, 1961. Paper.

Riley, Matilda White; Johnson, Marilyn; and Foner, Anne (eds.). *Aging and Society*. New York: Russell Sage Foundation, 1968–72. 3 vols.

Rogers, Donald I. *Teach Your Wife to Be a Widow*. New York: Holt, 1953.

Rosenthal, Sylvia. *Live High on Low Fat*. Philadelphia: Lippincott, 1968. Paper.

Ryan, Kenneth J., and Gibson, Don C. (eds.). *Menopause and Aging*. Bethesda: U.S. Department of Health, Education, and Welfare, 1971. DHEW Publication No. (NIH) 73–319.

Schein, Clarence J. *A Surgeon Answers: 800 Questions and Answers About Surgery*. New York: Putnam, 1973.

Soddy, Kenneth, with Kidson, Mary C. *Men in Middle Life*. Philadelphia: Lippincott, 1967.

Statistical Abstract. See U.S. Bureau of the Census.

Stetson, Damon. *Starting Over*. New York: Macmillan, 1971.

Sullivan, Harry Stack. *The Interpersonal Theory of Psychiatry*. New York: Norton, 1953.

U.S. Bureau of the Census. *Statistical Abstract of the United States: 1973*. Washington, D.C., 1973.

U.S. Bureau of Labor Statistics, Department of Labor. *Employment and Earnings*, vol. 20, no. 7. Washington, D.C.: U.S. Government Printing Office, 1974.

———. *Employment and Unemployment in 1973* (Special Labor Force Report 163). Washington, D.C.: U.S. Government Printing Office, 1974.

U.S. Employment Standards Administration, Department of Labor. *Age Discrimination in Employment Act of 1967: Report of 1974, Covering Activities under the Act during 1973*. [Washington, D.C.: Department of Labor, 1974.]

U.S. Social Security Administration, Department of Health, Education, and Welfare. *Your Medicare Handbook*. Washington, D.C.: U.S. Government Printing Office, 1973.

Vedder, Clyde B. (ed.). *Problems of the Middle-Aged*. Springfield: Thomas, 1965.

Winch, Robert F., and Spanier, Graham B. (eds.). *Selected Studies in Marriage and the Family.* 4th ed. New York: Holt, 1974.

Wortis, Sam Bernard; Bond, Douglas D.; Braceland, Francis J.; Freedman, Daniel X.; Friedhoff, Arnold J.; and Lourie, Reginald S. (eds.). *The Year Book of Psychiatry and Applied Mental Health.* Chicago: Year Book Medical Publishers, 1970.

Zugibe, Frederick T. *Eat, Drink, and Lower Your Cholesterol.* New York: McGraw-Hill, 1963.

Zussman, Leon, and Zussman, Shirley. "Dual Sex Team Therapy of the Couple." To be published in *Cornell Seminars,* Brunner-Mazel, 1974.

Index